BEHIND the SMILE

Behind the Smile

A Survivor of the Métis Sixties Scoop

KP ROGERS

FOREWORD BY ALBERT BECK, SENIOR POLICY ANALYST, MÉTIS NATIONAL COUNCIL, OTTAWA, ON.

The views and opinions expressed in this book are those of the author and do not necessarily reflect those of the publisher, and the publishers hereby disclaim any responsibility for them.

All rights reserved, including the right to reproduce this book or portions thereof in any form whatsoever without written permission. For permission or information, contact

KP Rogers
kp.rogers.bts@gmail.com

Copyright © 2020 KP ROGERS
All rights reserved.
ISBN: 978650933168

Dedicated to all my relations- the tens of thousands of Indigenous children that were separated from their families and communities in the Sixties Scoop, and to the families that suffered their loss. May there be healing.

All my life people have nicknamed me Smiley. It became a notable occurrence. An acquaintance told me once that someone that smiles all the time has something to hide. My entire life has been about hiding my shame, pain and fear behind my smile.

Hence, I needed to write this book to climb out of the painful abyss that consumed my entire life. I wanted to show myself from behind the smile.

Acknowledgments

Writing my story helped me to get my thoughts out of my head and into print, where they are less problematic and painful.

I want to thank my friend I.B. for his encouragement for thirty years to write my story. I wish you were here to read the final chapter.

Likewise, thank you to the many friends and family that encouraged me over the years.

I want to give a very special thank you to my partner, Jack, who has put up with late, late nights, mood swings, and tears and who, through the whole process, has remained sane and supportive. You are one tough guy, babe.

Thank you to all my friends that beta read my work and provided support, perspective, and guidance: Faye D, Diane L, Lori E, Jean S, Jack F., and Albert B; I am grateful for all your ideas, and encouragement.

I am thankful that I was introduced to my mentor/publisher-assist, Kelly Falardeau of Mixx & Koki Publishing Bookkellytospeak@gmail.com. Thank you for your help, guidance, and input. Your critiques kept me focused. You are making me better.

To my ultra-talented editor – that I think of as a newfound friend – you are amazing. You made my work sparkle. Thank you, Patricia Ogilvie, Editor with ProriskEnterprises.com, so much. I was like an overdue first-time mother – you were my midwife!

Thank you to Vikki at VC_BookCovers, http://vcbookcovers.com for the awesome job of creating my book cover. It is like the wedding dress on the bride.

To my dear friend, Albert Beck. Thank you for supporting me in this process and agreeing to write a Foreword to this book. This has been a crazy wild year for me, as you know from the time we spent together in Richmond and at Back to Batoche Days. I look forward to many more get-togethers, my friend! Albert is available for speaking engagements. You can reach him at abeck202020@gmail.com.

Most of all, I want to thank – YOU – my reader. Seriously, I appreciate you more than you can know, and I am humbled that you invested your time and allowed me the privilege of entertaining you and perhaps educating you a little bit. Since reader reviews are very helpful for authors, let me know how this impacted you by going to Amazon and leaving a book review on my book. I hope we spend time together again. Until then, Happy Reading!

KP Rogers

Foreword

I am honoured to write this foreword for KP Rogers. Not only because like her, I am a Métis who survived the Sixties Scoop, but because I deeply believe that healing from trauma can manifest itself in many forms such as putting pen to paper. I repatriated with my Métis birth family in 1997 and I know the importance of putting to rest the demons that worked to destroy my physical, mental, emotional and spiritual self.

I am a Senior Policy Analyst and Senior Advisor to the Métis National Council's (MNC) Minister responsible for the Métis Nation's Sixties Scoop file. I met KP in April 2019. The MNC in partnership with the Métis Nation British Columbia hosted an engagement session to seek advice on the best way to reconcile the wrongs of the Sixties Scoop for Métis Nation Survivors. We met again in July 2019 at the Métis Nation's annual Back to Batoche Festival in Saskatchewan. We shared stories of our experiences over a snack and agreed to keep in contact by phone and email. And like the Métis Nation's flag, our bond is unbreakable and for infinity.

What is the Sixties Scoop? The author of the 1983 report *Native Children and the Child Welfare System*, Patrick Johnson coined the term Sixties Scoop. The term refers to a time in Canadian history when First Nation (Treaty and non-Treaty Indians), Inuit and Métis children were "scooped" (removed by state authorities) from their families. Many were illegally placed in non-Indigenous families in Canada, the United States and overseas. Now as adults, many survivors suffer debilitating mental and physical health illnesses. Almost all have lost their connection to Indigenous spirituality and ceremonies that have led to an emotional disconnection from self and the world that then acts as fuel for premature death and suicide.

"Scooping" continues today among First Nation, Inuit and Métis children in Canada. Dr. Jacqueline Marie Maurice has coined this continued phenomena as the *Millennium Scoop*.

Behind the Smile emanates from the lived experiences of KP Rogers. Her story exposes a dark truth of the Canadian child welfare system and its genocidal treatment of the Métis Nation and its most important legacy—our children. Like many Métis families dealing with the aftermath of the fraudulent Métis Script System, KP articulates the harsh realities through the eyes of a child. She describes in great detail the struggles, survival tactics and fallout of those inequities that result in the deconstruction of her Métis family. KP weaves into her story experiences that capture your attention immediately with vivid memories that leave you wondering how these traumatic experiences could possibly be inflicted so harshly by individuals and institutions that had the best interest of the child.

You will experience a whole host of emotions making you wish that you could have done something to help prevent these traumatic experiences from ever happening. In all this chaos, KP shares one of her most intimate experiences with the world. She then demonstrates her resistance and resilience as a Métis woman by sharing how she worked to heal herself so that others who are going through the same or similar experiences can benefit and find their healing. *Behind the Smile* is a tribute to all women, Sixties Scoop Survivors, Métis people and the human spirit.

This book contributes to the healing narratives being expressed by Sixties Scoop Survivors all across Canada. I hope it will be the primer for your understanding of Métis who experienced severe trauma as a result of child welfare policies developed by Canadian governments. For those Survivors reading, I hope this book will act as a conduit for your healing journey and bring you out from behind your smile.

By Albert Beck

Table of Contents

ACKNOWLEDGMENTS	VI
FOREWORD	VIII
CHAPTER 1 -- IN HAPPIER TIMES	3
CHAPTER 2 -- LEFT BEHIND	19
CHAPTER 3 -- AUNTIE JEAN	32
CHAPTER 4 -- THE GRAHAMS	42
CHAPTER 5 -- A LITTER OF UNWANTED KITTENS	54
CHAPTER 6 -- MARLENE	58
CHAPTER 7 -- FOSTER HOME - MRS. E	66
CHAPTER 8 -- MR. E	104
CHAPTER 9 -- HEALING	123
CHAPTER 10 -- I AM MÉTIS	138
BIBLIOGRAPHY	148
ABOUT THE AUTHOR	149

Three Sisters 1958
Karrie – age 3, Lyndsay – age 1, Cindy – age 5

Chapter 1 — In Happier Times

When I was a little girl, my daddy bought me a rubber dolly, the kind with the porcelain face, and real human hair. She was the most beautiful doll I had ever seen, so much prettier than any of the dirty babies my little friends played with. Her eyes were delicately and intricately hand-painted jewels of sapphire blue. Each lash was perfectly placed and uniformly curled, giving her a look of purity and innocence. Her lips were soft and sweet with a slight pout, like the petals of a snapdragon, and her cheeks had a delicate blush, just like mine did when Daddy would stroke my hair and call me his little princess. I would imagine, as I lovingly played with Lucy, that this was how my Daddy was with me.

I would spend my days in make-belief, being a gentle and loving mommy with my beautiful, happy, and obedient 'daughter' Lucy. Life was a splendid and happy time, living in a fine mansion; brightly lit with grand chandeliers that cast their colored lights as the sun entered the huge windows and touched the crystals refracting speckles of dancing fairy lights on the brightly painted walls of pastel pink and soundlessly slipped across the plush pink carpets which ran all the way from wall to wall.

The rooms were filled with wonderful furniture of tables and chairs painted with gold trim. Not just painted on trim, but real gold trim that could be taken off to pay the maids and gardeners and given away to friends, but grew back each day, like magic. The couches and chairs and bed linens were all of the finest, softest fabric with bright pink flowers. It all smelled like pink flowers.

And every day, Daddy would come home and scoop me up in his arms as he planted kisses all over my face. I would see him as he twirled me around and around until I laughed with glee and felt slightly dizzy. Then he would throw himself into a chair, with me on his lap, clinging to his neck. With his blue eyes twinkling, he'd say, "Who is my favoritist little princess in the whole world?"

And I'd say, "I am Daddy! I am!"

***

That was my life in my make-believe world.

I am Daddy, I thought as I wrinkled my nose at the smell of piss and old clothes, and watched the dust specks sift dreamily toward the floor in the sunbeam in which I lay. I raised my arm and watched the specks swirl and dance crazily around and around until they disappeared outside the magical, invisible borders of the sunbeam. Sleepily I wondered where those funny little things went to so suddenly that I could no longer find them. I raised my gaze upward to the tiny window high above me between two bunk beds that took up most of the space in the dingy little room. The windowpane was thoroughly coated with a film that made the sky outside look dreary and grey even when it was bright and sunny. It cast haloes around the streetlights at night.

I hated days like this because I knew it was warm, and the sun was shining outside. I could vaguely hear children's voices as they squealed and sang in the playground across the street. But as usual, Mama was still asleep, and I was never allowed outside until she got up, and often that wasn't until long after lunchtime.

I sighed as I looked over to the 'lump' sleeping in one of the dresser drawers, which was pulled out and lying in the corner of the closet. This was my baby sister Lyndsay, and this was her bed. Somehow Lyndsay[1] reminded me of Lucy. I guess it was her snapdragon lips, which always made her look like she was pouting – even now as she slept peacefully. Her soft black hair felt so much like Lucy's; maybe it was even made from hers, I guessed.

Beside Lyndsay and almost hiding her in the closet, were stacks of clothes in various stages of disrepair tossed carelessly into cardboard boxes. The clothes spilled out of the broken sides of the boxes and lay strewn across the floor until someone kicked them back together and piled them in the corners of the closet. There they would stay until someone used the corner of the closet in a game of hide and seek, or more likely where four little brown faces would hide when the fighting would begin. That is why the boxes were so tattered

---

[1] Pseudonyms have been used throughout this book

and no longer concealed their contents; that is why the closet and its wretched contents smelled of stale piss.

The only other thing in the room was an old dresser with the bottom drawer missing and the face missing on the top drawer exposing its contents of little girls' panties and socks. The hole where the missing drawer was from, doubled as a garage where my older brother, Ronnie, parked his matchbox cars and trucks. With a little imagination, one could see the shoebox service station and matchbox gas pumps and roads which lead from everywhere to nowhere.

Ronnie was the oldest of us, at eight years, and in grade three. Cindy was six and in grade one. Each morning Ronnie would wake them up at seven and scrounge up something to eat or drink. Even at their young ages, Ronnie and Cindy ate their breakfasts in silence and left the house when the big hand on the clock was straight up, and the little hand was on the eight.

There would be a small plastic bowl left on the table for me. Sometimes it had a few flakes or grains of dry cereal; sometimes, it had dry, stale bread pulled apart to resemble cereal. Beside my bowl was a bottle of milk, or water if that was all there was, that I was supposed to feed to Lyndsay when she woke.

One day, while on their way to school, Ronnie and Cindy foolishly became lost in a game of exploring, and equally as lost in their track of time. That day they came home from school with a note from their teacher.

Mama's eyes narrowed, and her mouth drew into a straight line as she read the note.

"What were you two little bastards up to this morning?" Mama spat. She pulled back her yet uncombed hair with a shaky hand that gave away the truth of another rough night.

I knew that tone, and it frightened me. My eyes grew big as I dashed a glance at my brother and sister, who now had Mama's complete attention. I used this as an opportunity to steal away from the room and hide in the dark corner of the closet on top of smelly clothes.

"How many times have I told you to go straight to school?" I heard Mama yell.

"Answer me!" she roared.

"Lots I guess, Mama," Ronnie squeaked.

"I'm sorry, Mama," Cindy whimpered.

"Sorry huh? All the trouble and shit I get into because of you two! Do you know what you have done? What if they come and take you away? First your lame ass dad runs out on me and now all you can do is cause me trouble,"—she steamed on and on—"It would serve you right."

I started to see black things, like tiny black flies, getting thicker and thicker in my vision, until I could not see anything but black. Sounds began to move far away, like coming out of a black tunnel—*and I could see Daddy coming, swooping me up in his arms and saying, "Who is my favoritist little princess?"*

"*I am Daddy. I am!*" I cried as I pushed my face into my knees.

"—hold still you little bastard! I said, hold still!" Mama yelled.

I could hear her fists land on Ronnie's back and hear her palms smack on his face.

"Don't you move, bitch! You're next—"

Screaming, yelling, pleading, begging—all far away now.

"—*I am Daddy. I am!*" And then I was 'going.' I was going, and I couldn't stop. I whimpered at the thought of Mama finding out, and even then, my bladder made full release. I felt the clothes under me grow warm, and my socks get wet around my toes. Fear for myself rose and swallowed the anguish for my sister and brother. Was I next? Quietly, I crawled out of my hiding place in the shadowed corner of the closet. I slipped off the wet panties, threw them into the back of the closet, and climbed into dry ones from the pile of dirty clothes.

Ronnie and Cindy came into the little room with tears running down their faces, but neither of them dared to make a sound.

Mama had worn out her rage on them, but the slightest wrong move could send her back out of control. Mama had told them to keep "the other brats" quiet because their escapade had given her another headache. Her bedroom door slammed shut.

Ronnie and Cindy sat on the edge of the bed; Ronnie drew Cindy up close to him and put his arms around her. Both of their faces became expressionless. They looked like beaten animals as they silently waited for Mama to calm down and give them their reprieve – which was just as predictable as the punishment.

I crawled up on the bed and quietly took my place beside my brother and sister. I looked up into their faces and with a small smile, revealed to them the little presents I had hidden in my hands. We played silently with our toy cars and drove along roads that came from everywhere and lead to nowhere, and we played until it was time for them to go back to school.

The afternoon held no promise of getting any better. Lyndsay began to stir in her little bed. Mama had been up earlier that morning long enough to change Lyndsay's diaper and make a bottle which she handed to me. Although I was not much older than Lyndsay, I knew what to do with it. I had fed Lyndsay her bottle almost every morning since before she was a year old.

I guess it was a good thing Lyndsay usually slept all morning. But now she was awake, and I knew she would want more than just a bottle. And besides, she smelled bad. I sure hoped Mama would be feeling better soon because I had never changed Lyndsay's diaper and as much as I loved her, nor did

I want to. But as long as Mama's bedroom door was closed, I knew I had to keep Lyndsay quiet.

I peeked out the bedroom door into the kitchen. There should be some cookies in the top cupboard. I would need a chair for that, but I also knew Mama would be mad if I climbed on a chair to sneak cookies out of the cupboard; keeping Lyndsay quiet was more important now.

I was almost halfway across the room when I saw Alex, the big black and white tomcat, lying on the bulky, thread-bare red armchair in the corner between the kitchen and the living room.

Oh, how I hated that cat. If I caught his attention, I knew he would chase me. I don't know why he always chased me; I'd never done him any wrong. He never even noticed Ronnie or Cindy. So, silently and slowly, I tiptoed across the room to the chair that was standing close to the cupboard. I gave the chair a little push, and the legs scraped along the floor with a teeth-jarring screech.

I froze, then gave a glance at Mama's door, but I did not hear her stir, so I carefully tried again to move the chair. Finally, the chair was close enough to the cupboard, and up I climbed.

My luck was holding out. The cookie box was empty. I could hear Lyndsay in the bedroom beginning to wind up like a little engine. I had to find something fast. The crackers! That should work! I crouched down on the cupboard and stretched out my leg to find the edge of the chair behind me, and my heart leaped into my throat as my foot missed the chair, and I felt myself falling. I was already saying "ouch" before I even landed.

The chair fell over with a crash, and the dishpan full of dirty dishes crashed and clattered all over the floor. Now I was in trouble! Not only did Lyndsay choose this moment to find her full set of lungs, but I heard Mama's feet hit the floor as she leaped out of her bed.

"Karrie!" Mama gasped as she threw open her bedroom door and surveyed me laying on the floor in the midst of dirty dishes. "Karrie, what in the world are you doing? Are you OK?" Mama asked, with tenderness and concern evident in her voice. She quickly checked me over for obvious wounds.

I started to cry. Not because I was hurt, but because Mama actually sounded concerned. This was a different mama than the one that came out of her bedroom just a short time ago. This mama's face was softer; the voice was light as a song. She was not mad at me like the other mama would have been.

"Shhh, shhh, now baby. It's OK. Come here." Mama gently pulled me toward her and held me in her arms for a brief moment. "What were you doing? Were you up on the cupboard?" Mama asked me.

I gave my head a slight nod.

"Why?" she asked.

Mama was not always mean and angry. Just sometimes. This mama, I knew. This mama I loved, and I was not afraid of her. This mama was fun and funny sometimes. She was the one who played with us and read stories. This mama cuddled and snuggled with us kids. Sometimes she would lay on our bed in the dark and write our names with the lit tip of her cigarette. Sometimes we would play a game, and I would guess whose name she wrote by the swirls and flourishes of the glowing end of her cigarette.

Those were special times for me. But she was not always here, and I did not like the other one. When she talked or laughed too loud, her breath smelled just like that stuff in the bottle that she hid under her bed.

"I needed a cracker for Lyndsay so she wouldn't cry and wake you up," I said with my chin on my chest and my eyes looking at the floor.

"Hmmm, aren't you a good girl," she said as she picked me up in her arms and looked for the crackers.

Mama smelled of stale cigarettes and booze, with just a tiny residue of her perfume, and of course, the remnant scent of Mama underneath.

Finding the nearly empty saltine box, she pulled a few crackers out of the package. She poked one into my mouth and scrunched her nose at me and smiled. I smiled back and took the second one she offered me in my hand.

Mama placed me on the floor and popped a cracker into her mouth and took another with her into the bedroom. I stood beside the cupboard, nibbling the cracker, edges first. I listened as Mama chattered and cooed at Lyndsay while she changed her diaper and returned to the kitchen with Lyndsay propped on her hip. Lyndsay sucked on the edges of the cracker, creating a gooey mess.

It was a marvel at how quickly Mama could vanquish Lyndsay's complaints. But then Mama could put most people at ease if they gave her a chance. Especially the men who had recently started coming around at night and taking Mama out. I never saw them. But I heard them. And I hated them because after they left, the mean mama was sure to come back.

"Are you hungry, Karrie?" Mama smiled at me.

For the first time today, my stomach relaxed enough to let me know how hungry I was. I wiped my eyes with the back of my hands. I nodded my head.

"Ok. Come on. Let's get some clothes on you. Then after you have some lunch, you can go outside and play," Mama said with a smile.

I wonder where Mama went at night when she would spend so much time looking in the mirror and making herself pretty. She would call me to her room in the evening, and I would watch in awe as she would transform herself from just my mama into a radiantly beautiful woman. In my eyes, Mama was always pretty, but on these nights, she was really magnificent. She was even prettier than those flashy ladies in the magazines that Mama would buy every week at the corner store.

As happy as I was when I knew Mama was happy, I had an uneasy feeling in the pit of my stomach that told me these men were trouble.

How I wished that Daddy was here. Things were different when he was home. Mama was different then, too. She used to look pretty every night. She would brush her raven hair until it shone and put her makeup on with care, and just a dash of that special perfume Daddy bought her when he had gone into Edmonton one time on his way home from work.

Daddy worked for the Department of Highways and was gone away from home a lot. We all missed him when he was gone. Especially Mama, I think. But when he came back home for a while, the fighting would again become as common as the drinking. And then, once again, there would be peace and relief in the house when he left for work.

But it was times like now when Daddy had been gone a long time, and Mama was going out almost every night that I would forget what it was like after Daddy returned. I missed him. We all missed him.

Mama pulled out a pair of too-small shorts and a matching T-shirt and tossed them on the bed. "You can get dressed by yourself. I'll get a sandwich for you." Mama leaned over and picked up Lyndsay before she left the room.

I could hear her rummaging through the cupboards for the fixings of a sandwich, as I quietly slipped into my shorts and T-shirt.

Blah, peanut butter! I thought as I crinkled up my nose in a valiant effort to show disapproval to the sandwich Mama handed me. I hated peanut butter!

There were enough times that we had very little to eat, even times when the cupboards and fridge were completely bare. These were the times that Ronnie would pick flower buds, or the little yellow buds on the small fern-like weeds in the yard and put them in a plastic bowl for us to eat. We ate them without complaint. They were better than the discomfort of an empty stomach.

"Well, darling. I'm afraid that is all there is today," Mama said sadly. "If you are a good girl, you can sit out on the step and eat it before you go to play."

It was a small reward, but it worked. I took the sandwich and waited at the door for Mama to unlock and open the door for me. Another rule. I was never allowed out of the house until Mama opened the door for me.

I played in the small playground across the street until I saw Ronnie and Cindy walking toward me on their way home from school.

Mama came outside with a big smile on her face. "Tonight, we are going to have a very special night together!" she proclaimed to us. "So, everyone think real hard what you really, really want to do. Something special for each of you, ok?"

Ronnie was the first to answer, and he wanted to play soccer. It was his favorite thing to do, so Mama and Ronnie played soccer together. Cindy and I cheered as Ronnie made a score on Mama.

Then Mama played dollies with Cindy and me because that was what Cindy wanted to do.

"Now, Karrie, what do you want to do?"

"I just want to watch you get pretty."

At first, Mama did not understand, but then her face broke into a smile, and I knew she understood.

"Well, let's see." Mama thought for a moment. "While I have a quick bath, why don't Cindy and Karrie go to the store and get some eggs, and I will make egg foo yung for supper." We all cheered and hopped up and down. Chinese food was our favorite meal, and Mama was the best Chinese food cook in town. Everyone said so.

Ronnie watched over Lyndsay while Mama had a bath. Cindy and I ran to the corner store to get a dozen eggs with the money Mama had given Cindy.

When we arrived at the store, Mr. Hansen was busy with another customer. He had always been really friendly with us, but today when he finished with the other customer, he turned his back on us and started to rearrange things on the shelf behind him.

Finally, Cindy spoke up, "Mr. Hansen?"

He turned around to face us then and looked a little embarrassed. "Now look here, kids. You can't get anything here anymore unless you have money."

"We got money!" Cindy said as she showed him the two shiny quarters.

"I see. Well, what would you like then?" he softened.

"Mama needs some eggs," Cindy murmured.

Mr. Hansen turned away and made his way to the back of the small, overcrowded convenience store. He returned with a carton of eggs and thrust them at Cindy. "Get going now." He waved away the quarters. It was not the first time he had done so. It was not Mr. Hansen that minded giving us a few groceries; it was Mrs. Hansen.

When we arrived back home, Mama had finished her bath and had passed Lyndsay through the tub after her. Ronnie dried Lyndsay, and got her dressed in clean pajamas, while Cindy helped me take my turn in the tub. When I was clean and dry, I got dressed in pajamas and went to sit with Mama as she brushed her hair until it shone and carefully applied her makeup.

Cindy, then Ronnie, bathed in the same little galvanized tub that sat on the kitchen floor. We had all shared the same water, and it was the last person to bathe that had tepid and murky water. But we were all clean.

There was lots of laughter at our supper table that night. It was special, like it was a celebration of someone's birthday, like a party, almost. It has been a good day, after all!

Later that night, long after all us kids were in bed, I awoke to a strange voice in the house.

Chapter 2 — Left Behind

The late 1800s two-bedroom bungalow that we lived in was constructed of rough sawn lumber with newspaper and sawdust for insulation. It was humble in stature, and nothing pretty to look at, but no more so than any other house in the small town in the Alberta prairies in 1959. What was unusual about this house were the occupants: a single woman with four children – each with a different father. That was bad enough. What was worse than her questionable lifestyle was the fact that Marlene was a Métis woman, a breed woman, as the gentile women of the town referred to her.

Marlene was a beauty, for sure. A young Liz Taylor with brown eyes. She possessed the kind of beauty that men were inclined to chase, and women were inclined to despise. Marlene had no shortage of male company but never a lady friend to share her thoughts and feelings with. And whether it was a male or a female, no one would trust Marlene for more than a short time.

Finding a man was never a problem for Marlene. There were lots of men that came visiting at our house. The lucky ones took what they came for and left. The ones that stayed too long became our next daddy, and the father of the next baby.

The interior walls had no insulation to afford a level of privacy, so I could hear clearly the whispered tones coming from the next room.

Try as I might, I could not figure out who the male voice belonged to. His voice was deep, and it rumbled, making me shiver. It was clear that he was angry.

One thing was certain; this was trouble. Mama was crying and pleading. She seemed to cry a lot lately. The two voices, hushed and raised, like a hum without a rhythm muffled through the wall. Her voice pleading and crying, his voice rumbling.

"Please…please no! Don't make me do this!" Mama cried, "I just can't!" Mama's voice was intense with emotion.

"Well, what about Shelly?" I heard his voice demand.

"Oh, for god-sake, she is just a kid herself! What could she possibly do with a bunch of kids?" Mama cried.

"Well then, there is only one alternative – Jean!" he snarled. "Make up your mind, Marlene. You know you can't stay here. Not since Wayne got that letter. He is jealous and he made a phone call to the welfare. He said if you are still here when he gets back on the weekend, he would kill you. And you know that he very well might. He nearly did the last time he was home. This is not going to end well either way"

"Maybe I can make a deal with him! These are his children too, and I'm sure that even if he could care less about me, he wouldn't want them to be homeless. He was just mad when he made that call to welfare. Maybe…"

"Are you nuts, Marlene? You don't want these kids anywhere near him, not that he would want them anyway! Besides, not all of them are his, remember. What would he do with a bunch of kids?"

"Well, what you are proposing isn't right either! I can't do it—I won't do it!" Mama tried reasoning, then implored.

"You will do it! You don't have a choice, now do you? What else are you going to figure out before Friday? Time is running out. Now make up your mind, Marlene. You can't stay here, and I am not going to be saddled with a bunch of kids. Maybe one, but not all of them! Maybe we can come back for them when we get settled." He lied. "Make up your mind. I'll be here early in the morning."

The bedroom door opened, a black shadow slipped across the floor, and out the door. Mama was still crying when I finally drifted back to sleep.

Morning came suddenly to the little house on the edge of town. I was not prepared for it. The night seemed to have been very short with all the dreams that had wrestled in my head all night. They left me feeling tired, confused, and nervous. It was barely more than dawn, and much earlier than our normal wake up time when Mama came into our room and quietly shook Ronnic, Cindy, and me out of our sleep. It was evident that Mama had not gone to bed last night. Her makeup was worn off, and her hair was uncombed. Her eyes were red-rimmed and puffy, so I knew she had been crying.

Just seeing her that way told me things were not right. Something was very wrong. But what? I knew better than to ask Mama. She told us the things that she wanted us to know, but not the things we asked about.

Mama motioned us to be quiet and pointed at our clothes to get dressed. We silently obeyed. When fully dressed, we came out of the dark bedroom and closed the door leaving Lyndsay alone and undisturbed.

Once in the kitchen, Mama placed bowls of dry puffed wheat in front of us for breakfast. Again, there was no milk for cereal, only a little left for a bottle for Lyndsay when she woke up. I wrinkled my nose at the cereal, but I had learned long ago not to refuse what was placed before me. However, it is still important to wrinkle your nose.

As I looked around the kitchen and living room, I noticed that it looked strangely different than it did the night before. It looked bare and clean. Things were missing.

"Hurry now, kids!" Mama said as she swept through the kitchen from her bedroom with a box in her arms. At the doorway, she handed the box to a man I had not seen before. "We are going on a holiday!"

"On a holiday?" asked Ronnie suspiciously. "Where we going to Mama?"

"You will see soon enough," Mama said brightly, without even glancing at us.

"Are we going to Grandma's?" I asked as I poked another puffed wheat into my mouth.

"No. Not to Grandma's." Mama answered.

"Is Daddy coming too?" I questioned.

"No," Mama said quietly.

"Where are we going, Mama?" I asked again.

"Just away for a holiday, OK? Now no more questions," Mama said, ending the discussion.

As soon we were all finished our breakfast, Mama combed our hair and told us to sit on the front steps. The last thing she did before we left was get Lyndsay out of bed, changed her diaper, and dressed her. Cindy got Lyndsay's bottle out of the fridge, and Mama grabbed the puffed wheat bag off the table. We all headed for Mama's friend's car that was parked beside the house.

The tall stranger had been standing beside the car since we got up, except for a few trips to the doorway to get the boxes that Mama handed to him. He had simply stood beside his car, smoking one cigarette after the other and looking anxiously around him.

Mama locked the back door and climbed into the front seat of the car next to the stranger. She held Lyndsay on her lap, and Cindy sat next to her. If Cindy sat up straight, she could look out the window and watch the fields and houses go by.

There were boxes packed in the back seat completely covering the floor and seat, right to the roof, with just enough room for Ronnie and me to squeeze in.

The tension was high in the air. Mama wasn't speaking at all, and even though nothing had really been said, I knew that something was wrong. My tummy was turning over, and I felt sick. I looked over at Ronnie. His eyes were wide, and his mouth was drawn in a straight line. He looked pale, and his freckles stood out on his nose and cheeks. He stared straight ahead and said nothing. I did the same.

The stranger started the engine and pulled the car out of the driveway and turned it down the street toward the highway. Once on the highway, he lit up another cigarette. He smoked it down to the filter and lit another one. Before we had travelled a half hour, he had smoked three cigarettes. The air was now blue with smoke, and it was hard to breathe in the little hole within the boxes where Ronnie and I sat. I knew exactly how Cindy felt when she suddenly began to wretch.

"Oh, Arvin, pull over! Quick, quick, quick!" Mama shouted in concern.

So, his name is Arvin, I thought.

As soon as the car stopped, Mama pushed the door open and carried Cindy to the side of the road. Cindy's face was chalky white. She was sweaty and hot. Cindy began to whine and cry.

"Great," Arvin grumbled. But that was all he said.

Mama had Cindy cleaned up and was back in the car now. She passed Lyndsay back to Ronnie and me, and Cindy lay down on the front seat with her head on her lap. The decision was finally made for Mama. She couldn't possibly leave a sick child behind. Jean would have a fit.

Time slipped away. It seemed like we were in Arvin's car for nearly an eternity. The purr of the engine and the warmth of the sun through the windows worked its spell, and soon all of the kids in the back seat were asleep. The next thing I knew, the car had stopped.

Mama turned her head and looked in the back seat at her three sleeping children. Tears began to well up in her eyes.

"Now, Marlene! Get hold of yourself! It will only make it worse," Arvin said impatiently.

With that, Mama set her jaw and squared her shoulders. In a cold voice, she told Ronnie and me to get out of the car and follow her to the house. She opened the car door and picked up Lyndsay. When I stepped out of the car and looked around, I did not recognize where we were.

We were parked in a driveway beside a big house covered with blueish grey asphalt shingles for siding. Bordering the driveway was a row of caragana trees. They were left to grow wild and created almost a shaded tunnel effect down the driveway.

Mama circled around to the back of the house. Ronnie and I followed obediently. Without knocking, she opened the door and walked in. We entered into a cool, dreary little kitchen with pretty curtains on the small window over the sink. The curtains stood out from the rest of the run-down place. The counters were worn-out yellow Formica with grey speckles, and a dull aluminum trim along the edge. There was a small grey-top table with chrome legs and four matching chairs with tattered plastic seats.

Mama silently reached up into the freezer compartment of the refrigerator and took out two popsicles. She handed one to Ronnie, and when she had broken the second one in two, she handed half to me and the other half to Lyndsay.

She told us to sit down on the floor and eat the popsicles and that Auntie Jean would be here soon. She simply turned around and walked out of the house. A moment later, we heard the car back out of the driveway.

I looked bewildered at Ronnie. What I saw frightened me more than Mama walking away. Ronnie did not look the same. He seemed older, somehow. Cold. Expressionless. All of a sudden, I wanted to sit on his knee. Everything was wrong. I felt hot. I felt ill. My tummy crawled. I wanted to cry, but I couldn't. I felt like I couldn't breathe, but I was. I closed my eyes. *I could see Daddy—he was coming through the door— "Who is my favoritist little princess?"*

"I am Daddy—I am."

"Karrie! Karrie!" Ronnie hissed, as he shook me. I heard a deep sob. It was me.

Behind the Smile

"Come here!" Ronnie said as he gathered Lyndsay and me closer to him.

We sat together on the floor until the popsicles melted.

Suddenly, Ronnie stood up and took Lyndsay's hand and reached for mine. "Come on, Karrie! Let's go."

"But Mama said to stay here. If we go, how will she find us?" I felt confused. Mama had said straight out to stay there. Ronnie knew he must always obey Mama. He rarely disobeyed her, and when he did, it was always followed by punishment.

"Never mind!" Ronnie snapped, "We are going home."

With that, I felt much better. I reasoned to myself that Ronnie was the oldest, and he knew what we should do. I knew he would take care of us, and at that moment, a new sense of trust for Ronnie came over me. In some way, Ronnie had just replaced Mama and Daddy.

Ronnie retraced our steps to where we got out of the car, with Lyndsay and me in tow. Sure enough, the car was gone. And with it, Mama and Cindy. Why had Mama just left us here? Why did she take Cindy with her?

I felt so confused that it became too much for me to even think about it anymore. So, I didn't. I just followed Ronnie and did what he told me to.

—and I saw Daddy—he came home—and he picks me up and twirls me around. "Who is my favoritist little princess in the whole world?" Daddy said. And his blue eyes twinkled."

And I daydreamed of playing with my daddy and my precious doll Lucy. How safe and wonderful were my fantasies. Here, I was safe! Here, all my dreams come true, and we were back at home in our big mansion, all of us together!

"Hurry up, Karrie!" Ronnie said in exasperation. For heaven sake, Lyndsay is doing better than you. Watch where you are going! You're going to step in a puddle and get your shoes wet!"

With the accumulation of stress over the past few days, the anger and frustration in Ronnie's voice was the last straw. All my nervousness, all the anxiety, all the queasy feeling in my tummy finally caught up with me, and it all crashed down on me. Like a tidal wave it crushed me to the ground. Huge racking sobs choked me. Tears started coming to my eyes. I brushed them away with the backs of my hands. I was sobbing, huge racking sobs shook my shoulders and made my stomach muscles ache for release. I couldn't see or even sense anything around me. It was like I was buried under a ton of warm water. It was sucking the air out of my lungs. I couldn't breathe anymore. My head started to spin. My face turned hot, and my nostrils turned cold. Finally, a sob broke, and I could breathe again, and I could hear again.

"Karrie! Karrie!" Ronnie was shouting as he shook me. "Karrie, stop it. I'm sorry! I'm sorry I yelled at you! Please stop crying," he said soothingly as he put his arms around me protectively and stroked my hair. Tears were streaming down his face. I could hear Lyndsay crying behind Ronnie.

So, there we sat. The three of us huddled together in each other's arms, and we cried – cried until all our tears were spent. Ronnie told us that he was going to take care of us now. He told us that we never had to worry because he was going to take care of us. He told us that everything was going to be OK now. His voice was soft, and his words were soothing. And I trusted him. I trusted him now, like I did Daddy.

Ronnie got to his feet again; Lyndsay and I followed suit. He looked around us as if he was getting his bearings straight. He was trying to retrace the direction we came in the car. He took my hand, and I took Lyndsay's hand, and we started to walk.

As we walked along, we began to talk about Mama and Daddy and about home. We played little games and had little adventures in the ditches along the sides of the streets. Eventually, our path led us all the way through the town, until we were walking in the ditches along the highway. Time was ours now, and we were at peace. We were closed off, together, inside our own little world.

Ronnie showed us where the field mouse trails were in the tangled dead grass. We discovered that if we followed the trails, we could sometimes get a glimpse of the fat field mice as they scrambled away from us and ran through small clearings into their tunnels. We saw hubcaps that had fallen off of passing vehicles as they sped along the highway just above us. The hubcaps were full of water that had little creatures swimming hither-dither, going nowhere. We even found an old car tire in the ditch. Ronnie turned it over, exposing a damp, yellow spot beneath it. There were all kinds of bugs and worms scurrying to get out of the bright sunlight.

It was warm and sunny and peaceful in the ditch as we played and made up stories and tales and adventures as we made our way along.

Sometime later we came to a service station on the side of the highway. We were hot and tired and thirsty by now. The dried grass in the ditches was laden with dust, so by now we were covered with a layer of grey dust. Tear streaks coursed down our cheeks, where the dirt had caked to our faces after we had our cry. Although we had been walking for quite some time, we had actually only travelled a distance of about two miles.

Ronnie told me to sit down on the curb in front of the gas station and keep an eye on Lyndsay. He told me he was going to go and phone Mama to come and get us.

I watched him as he approached a man in oil spattered dark green coveralls. They spoke for a couple of minutes before disappearing into the service station. In just a few minutes, Ronnie and the man reappeared and walked toward us. They were carrying bottles of pop and chocolate bars for all of us. This was a treat too good to imagine.

Behind the Smile

The man looked down at us with kind eyes and smiled as he handed us the welcome pop. Turning his head, the man smiled sadly at Ronnie and said, "OK, son, I'll go call your mother for you now. You just stay here, and I'm sure she will be along soon."

The waiting was now quite bearable since we had finished the pop and ate all the chocolate bars. We were just quietly and patiently waiting for Mama to come and get us. I was beginning to get sleepy, sitting in the warm sun, with my tummy full and happy.

I looked over at Lyndsay, who was nodding off, sitting upright on the curb. I moved closer to her and gently lowered her head down onto my lap. She jerked to awareness as her body started to move. "Shhhh," I soothed as she settled into my lap. With Lyndsay settled and asleep, I began to nod off as well.

A pair of big hands soon awakened me, gently lifting me into a police cruiser.

The station attendant with the kind eyes had not called Mama. Instead, he called the police. I didn't realize then that we would never see Mama again. I didn't even care. I just curled up on the back seat of the police cruiser and went to sleep.

I was four years old.

Chapter 3 — Auntie Jean

Although it was a warm spring day, it felt cool in the car when I awoke. The police cruiser was parked in the shade of the caragana trees in the driveway of the same house mama had dropped us at. A jolt of panic brought me quickly out of my sleep. I felt disoriented at first; so much had happened since mama shook me awake so early that morning. As I looked around, I saw Ronnie leaning against the car door, vigilantly watching our surroundings. Just the sight of him caused me to relax, and when I noticed Lyndsay lying on the seat beside me, I relaxed further.

A police officer was sitting in the front seat on the passenger side. He turned his head to look at us in the back seat, but I snapped my eyes closed and pretended to be asleep.

We waited in the car for quite a while, Ronnie keeping watch, the police officer glancing back and me pretending to be asleep. Presently, a bulky squat woman came ambling down the driveway. I heard muffled voices outside the car as another police officer that I had not noticed until now, stopped the woman. I could hear voices speaking to each other; voices raised and lowered, sometimes angry, sometimes appeasing, clearly in deep discussion about something. I heard the woman mention Marlene, and I heard Ronnie's name and Lyndsay's name, and Karrie. That was me. They were arguing about us.

I didn't care. As long as Ronnie was here, I didn't care. I was sure that everything would be OK because Ronnie promised that he would take care of us.

The police officer and the woman went into the house, and quite some time later, she came back out with the officer and opened the back door of the police cruiser. Ronnie held onto my hand while the policeman that had been sitting in the front seat of the car came to the back door and gently picked up Lyndsay. When Ronnie and I stepped around the car, I recognized the woman right away. It was Auntie Jean.

We followed the adults into the small house with the asphalt shingle siding. I thought how strange it was that we were right back here. The police left. I guess all the discussions and arrangements concerning us three kids were made, without a question asked of us, nor an explanation given. We stayed together, always touching or huddled close, and silently watched and listened.

There were lots of angry words and questions discussed around us that night. Just before supper time, Auntie Jean's husband, Harry, came home from work. There had been no warning that there were three new little mouths in the house. It seemed that no amount of explaining from Auntie Jean could help him to understand what we were doing there and what he was supposed to do about it. He was not happy.

Just as the supper dishes were put on the table, the door banged open, and two teenagers, one boy and one girl shuffled into the house. They did not even see us sitting on the floor just inside the living room. More discussions and more angry words were spoken as we sat on the floor and watched the four of them eat supper. They talked about us kids and the situation they were in and angrily threw around the name Marlene. They threatened each other, cussed and swore, whined, and eventually, the dinner dishes were stacked in the sink. Auntie Jean huffed out a big sigh and called us into the kitchen.

She handed us each a piece of bread with a skiff of margarine, which we all ate silently. Auntie Jean gave Lyndsay a small glass of watered-down milk. There was no bottle for Lyndsay, so I guess it was time for her to learn to drink from a glass. She was, after all, nearly three years old. We needed her to stop being a baby, and I guess when we stopped treating her like one, she stopped acting like one.

That was our first night without our mother. She was gone. She had left us. None of us cried for her. I think we missed her, but everything was so strange and strained, with new rules to learn and live by, that we had little time to lament our loss. Besides, this was just temporary, right?

But I thought about it from time to time. Why had she left us? Why did she take Cindy with her? Where did they go? What had we done wrong? One thing was for sure; it was my fault. But how could she leave sweet little Lyndsay? She was just a baby still on the bottle. How could Mama choose one and leave the rest? Why did she punish Lyndsay and Ronnie when it was all my fault?

I would never understand. I knew I would never forgive Mama. I had forgiven her for all the long silent mornings of trying to keep Lyndsay satisfied and quiet, all the lonely scary nights when Mama was gone, and we were home alone – all the times that she raised her hand against any one of us. I always forgave Mama. But on this day, a painful stain colored my heart, and I felt the bitter root of unforgiveness twine its icy fingers into my heart.

It seems strange. But it is a truth for certain. It is the events of the greatest sorrow in one's life that create a memory of the most profound clarity in one's mind.

We were exhausted by the events of a very long and emotional day. When we were all placed on the couch in the living room and a blanket thrown over us, we fell asleep immediately.

The next morning, we stayed huddled together on the couch until Auntie Jean called us into the kitchen. She handed us each a piece of dry toast that had been left over from their breakfast. She sent us outside and told us to sit on the back steps until she called for us. We ate the toast in silence. It was still more than we often had at home.

As I ate, I looked around the back yard. There was a large green building at the far end of the property. The caragana trees that grew into a tunnel along the driveway in the front of the house carried on along the border of the property, turned left, and grew up against the back of the green building at the back of the property. The building had large overhead doors on both ends and a smaller man door beside each of them. Although I couldn't see them from the back steps, the far side of the building had a row of windows that were about three feet up from the ground.

There were raised rabbit hutches on the left side of the yard. I could see the fluffy animals bouncing around in the pens, and I was itching to play with them. I had never seen real bunnies before, but Mama had read us stories about Peter Rabbit and Thumper.

I could hear Auntie Jean talking on the phone. She talked to many different people that morning. At lunchtime, she came out and gave us another piece of bread with margarine and told us to go play in the yard. She told us not to leave the yard, and never to look in the windows of the green building. She left us there to take care of ourselves while she went off to spend the afternoon at the bar. Auntie Jean had not seen a completely sober day in any number of years that even she could not recall. Clearly, the three of us were not about to change that pattern.

We were very happy to be left alone. We explored the back yard and spent a lot of time pulling grass to feed the rabbits. Ronnie found us a hiding place where we would be safe, just in case. He told us that if we were ever scared or in trouble that we were supposed to sneak there and hide and that he would come and find us. I understood.

There were no more beatings while we were at Auntie Jean's house. We were not a welcome addition to her family, and we were treated very separately while we were there. We never ate with them at the table but sat on the kitchen floor and ate after they had eaten and gone their separate ways. It didn't mean anything to us. We did not belong here, but we knew that. It all seemed emotionless, but that didn't matter either because we had each other – the three of us, and that was all we needed – that and the bread and toast that we ate.

Auntie Jean had managed to snag Harry, a lumbering oaf of a man, in marital bliss. Bliss because although he could not recall his last sober day, he had managed to provide a semblance of livelihood at a machine shop at the edge of the town of Leduc. There he worked with tools, washed his massive mitt-like paws in gallons of motor oil, wiped them on tattered old coveralls coated in the black foul-smelling stuff, and then return to the bar each night before he staggered home in time to eat and slump into his bed.

Jean and Bubbs, as they called Harry, had managed to propagate a reflection of themselves – a boy, a miniature sullen Bubbs, and a girl, a slightly loftier, albeit sober image of Jean. I never knew their names. It was not important; they never spoke to us or acknowledged we were there. Neither did Bubbs.

I had found the little trail that ran behind the green building in the back of the yard, the caragana trees growing up behind the building, creating a delightful shady tunnel that was just perfect for little people to run back and forth through it. We didn't have any toys to play with, but I had a fertile imagination. I saw mysterious lands, kind of like Alice in Wonderland when I looked down the tunnel. I could feel the breeze rush through my bangs like the mane on the horse I would become as I galloped or pranced down the tunnel. It was my favorite play place.

One day I noticed some older kids go into the green building. I went to the back and looked down the tunnel. I know that I had been told never to look into the windows, but that was a long time ago. This day, I forgot. I sneaked to the window in the middle of the building, and standing on my tiptoes, I peeked into the building.

I saw the boys run for the back door. I'd been caught. I was scared, and I started to run down the tunnel to get to Ronnie, who was playing with the rabbits. I had to get to him. As I cleared the tunnel, the boys burst through the back door. They chased me across the yard and caught me just before I got to Ronnie.

That day, two of the boys held me. Another one raised a gun and shot. The sound of the gun and the sound of the blood whooshing through my inner ears merged. A red mist covered my eyesight, and a pounding buzz blocked out my ears. Each heartbeat was measured in minutes as I slowly collapsed on the ground. I could see every face before me twist in horror. Someone started to scream – a long, muffled scream. My eyes slowly moved the length of my leg to the torn red spot on my ankle. It was then that I first felt the pain.

I suddenly realized it was me that was screaming. Hysterically I searched the yard for Ronnie. The world exploded in a flash of light and then went black. I was lying on the ground when my vision cleared.

I saw Ronnie. He was frozen in place; his eyes were glazed and unseeing. His hands held the body of a rabbit as it struggled to free itself from his stranglehold on the creature's neck. It seemed like minutes passed. Very slowly, like a movie in slow motion, Ronnie started toward me. The lifeless body of the rabbit fell at his feet.

I closed my eyes and allowed the hum to fill my head—*and I saw Daddy coming toward me. He had a big smile on his face, and his arms were outstretched to me. I climbed up on his knee, and he stroked my hair and said, "Who is my favoritist princess in the whole world?"*

And I said, "I am Daddy. I am."

I don't recall anything else that day. All I remember is being with Daddy, and that everything was OK. I wasn't unconscious; I wasn't asleep. I just wasn't there.

The bullet shattered my ankle bone. It eventually would heal. But the bullet also simultaneously shattered something inside both my child-sized psyche and Ronnie's. That would take much longer to heal. The suffering that attached two children with an unbreakable bond, that only enduring more than what was fair for any child to be put through, culminated that day in a tornado of emotion that was thoroughly and mercilessly unleashed. It could likely never be clearly attributed to this one single event, but something was thrown into the wind that day that would be reaped other days, years, to come in both our lives.

Somehow Ronnie got blamed for shooting me and for strangling the rabbit. No one cared about the truth.

My ankle, bound up in a big bandage which hid the damage, and outside of my limp, the matter seemed soon to be forgotten. At least it was no longer found in every conversation in one way or another.

Even I soon forgot the matter. But Ronnie never did. He was at my bedside when I went to sleep at night and there again when I woke up. He brought me water to drink and helped me get around. Our bond grew ever closer, and I truly depended on Ronnie for everything.

Although I heard the commands of Auntie Jean or someone else, it was Ronnie that I listened to. And when he stopped what he was doing and looked straight into my eyes and told me I had to be very good and not disobey the rules, I listened. I did not want to bring any more trouble onto Ronnie like he got the day I got shot. Everyone was yelling at Ronnie.

I never understood why, because it was me that had caused all the trouble. But I vowed to myself that I would be very good and do what I was told so that Ronnie did not get into any more trouble because of me. I was afraid that if I caused him trouble that he would go away and leave me too. Just like Daddy did. Just like Mama did.

Chapter 4 — The Grahams

Several times after that, Ronnie would gather up Lyndsay and me, and we would run away, only to be brought back and punished. The truth was, we did not want to be part of this family. We did not belong. We did not want to belong. We were homesick and needed our mother.

We had rules, but there was seldom anyone around to supervise us. We were simply expected to follow the rules.

It was not many weeks later, and Auntie Jean and Bubbs had endured all they could from Marlene's brats. That's what they called us. We were unwanted and uninvited intrusions in their lives. There was the constant fear that the scrutiny of the welfare would follow Marlene's kids to their doorway. It was an ever-present fear in Métis households in 1959.

One afternoon two strangers came to the back door and knocked. Auntie Jean invited them in. I hobbled behind Ronnie to the rabbit hutches. My leg was nearly healed and only had a small bandage on it. Auntie Jean scolded me often and told me that my ankle didn't hurt anymore and that I was just limping for sympathy.

"Does your foot hurt, Karrie?" Ronnie asked without looking up from feeding the rabbits long strands of grass he had pulled for them.

"Uhuh," I mumbled. "Who is that?" I did not have to specify. Ronnie knew who I meant. We were both wary of strangers.

"Dunno," he said. "But if they try to take one of us away, promise me you will run and hide. I'll come find you."

I was instantly frightened. Ronnie was bigger and older than me, and in my mind, he was brave and strong and smart. I knew he would always take care of Lyndsay and me. Like a dad.

"Are they going to take us away?" I asked in fear.

"Maybe," Ronnie said cautiously. "But if they take me away, you watch out for Lyndsay, OK?"

"I'm a-sccared, Ronnie," I stammered, through the tears that rose inside of me.

"I promise I'll come back for you. If they take me away, I'll come back for you and Lyndsay."

"But what if they take me away?" Since I was the one that caused all the trouble, it made more sense that they would take me away.

"They won't," he promised. Then seeing the fear and doubt in my eyes, he added, "but if they do, I'll find you. I promise, Karrie. Don't worry. We will always be together. I will always take care of you and Lyndsay."

Ronnie kept a close watch on the car that the two strangers arrived in. He was watching so they didn't sneak away with Lyndsay.

It was a hot and sunny Alberta afternoon. The kind of day that causes most to seek out the shade. Ronnie and I laid down on our stomachs under the rabbit hutches and kept guard over the strangers' car. We would be hidden from all but the most scrutinizing eyes, laying there in the cool and shade. But through the long blades of grass, we could see the whole back yard, and would know in advance if they tried to take Lyndsay away.

"Argh!" I cried as I shuffled backward away from the spider that was crawling down my arm off my sleeve.

Ronnie reached over and picked the bug up in his hand. "There is nothing wrong with him, chicken!" he giggled.

"I don't like them," I mumbled with a shudder that ran through my whole body. I clenched my teeth as Ronnie watched the bug with intrigue. Suddenly he stopped the spider with one leg. He slowly pulled until the leg fell off. Then another and another leg, each leg lay on the ground in front of Ronnie, still twitching. He had an oddly chilling smile on his face. I felt uncomfortable. The smile was out of place.

"It was only a daddy longlegs," Ronnie blandly stated when he noticed the look of disgust on my face. Ronnie's face had suddenly changed before my eyes. I had never noticed that before. But if I had to reflect back on it, I'd witnessed it happen before. I can't say I was frightened, but the scene was imprinted on my memory like a polaroid snapshot. It just now came into focus. The meaning of it came into focus much later.

We looked up as the back door squeaked open. Auntie Jean appeared in the doorway.

"Ronnie!" she called out. We sat as still as possible. I barely dared to breathe.

"Ronnie!" she shouted again. Still we never moved. Auntie Jean's eyes slowly scanned the yard.

I was sure she had missed us when her eyes scanned passed us the first time. I must have breathed.

Auntie Jean's eyes drew back to where Ronnie and I lay in the shadows under the rabbit cages. "I see you there, Ronnie! Answer me!" she said crossly.

"What?" Ronnie answered.

"Come here! Now!" she commanded.

I reached out and touched Ronnie.

He looked straight into my eyes, "I'll find you. I promise. Take care of Lyndsay."

The words filled my heart with dread and terror. I'd never been alone before. I'd always had Ronnie.

"Come here, right now, Ronnie!" Auntie Jean's voice carried with it the veiled threat. It meant to come here now, or else.

Ronnie stood up, slowly walked to the house, and disappeared inside. I never took my eyes off the door. Every minute seemed like an eternity.

Sometime later, Auntie Jean came to the door and called again, "Karrie, come on in here."

I leaped to my feet and ran across the yard to the back steps.

"Go on to the bathroom, girl, and wash your hands and face, and go pee."

I responded without question and obeyed to the letter. When I was finished with the bathroom, Auntie Jean shoved me into the small, windowless room behind the kitchen where Ronnie, Lyndsay, and I slept. It was actually the pantry, with shelves meant for food and cleaning supplies. A small bed had been squashed into the room; all three of us slept on the same bed.

On the bed was a cardboard box, and Auntie Jean began throwing our clothes into it. Ronnie was on the other side of the room, doing the same with his clothes. No one said a word. My heart began to slow down. I knew whatever was happening, it was happening to all three of us because all our clothes were being packed. When we finished putting our clothes in the box, Auntie Jean shooed us into the kitchen where the two strangers sat at the chrome-legged kitchen table, sipping coffee out of chipped mugs.

Auntie Jean spoke first. "Kids, this is Mr. Webster and Miss Benson. You are going for a ride with them." That was all she said.

"Hi," the young lady said with a bright smile. "You must be Karrie."

I simply nodded my head.

"And you must be Ronnie," she said as she turned toward my brother and smiled. Ronnie answered with a nod.

The man stood and stepped around us; he went into the bedroom; he reappeared with the two small cardboard boxes in his arms. Excusing himself as he tried to pass everyone in the small kitchen, he disappeared out the back door. A moment later, he returned.

"OK then," the man in the suit and tie said as he rubbed his hands together like he had unwanted dirt on them. "I guess that's all of it then. Miss Benson, do you want to go in and get the little one? You kids can come with me."

Everything the man said sounded like commands. Ronnie and I moved toward the door as he held it open for us. We stepped out the door and down the steps to the level of the yard. There we waited, hand in hand until the lady appeared carrying Lyndsay. We waited for her to pass us, then we followed her to the car and climbed into the back seat where she laid Lyndsay. Auntie Jean never followed us. She never said another word to us. Not even a wave goodbye. The last time I saw her, she was standing by her kitchen stove on a hot Alberta summer day. She was likely at the door of the bar before we hit the edge of Leduc town limits.

It didn't matter, though. We were still all together. The three of us. And that was all that mattered.

✦✦✦

We were taken to a small house in Wetaskiwin, Alberta. We were greeted by an older man and woman who beamed kindness from their whole faces. Their voices were kind; their actions were kind. They were introduced to us as Mr. and Mrs. Graham[2]. It took us a few days to settle in.

We had our own room at the top of a steep stairway on the second floor that was little more than an upgraded attic. There were two big beds, but we still all slept together in one bed anyway. The bedding was clean and smelled nice.

The entire house was tidy and clean. The furniture looked old and tired, like the Grahams. Each room was small – the house was the smallest one on the block. But the yard was pretty, an array of roses and flowers growing along the edge of everything: the fence, the house, the garage in the back. The yard exuded sunshine and smiles, like Mrs. Graham.

We sat at the table three times a day and ate as much as we wanted. We ate the same food that Mr. and Mrs. Graham ate. We had dessert with every dinner. We got to eat fruit, too. I felt safe and happy for the first time that I could remember.

Ronnie began smiling, and Lyndsay started to laugh and talk. Lyndsay's first words were spoken in this home.

Ronnie started school in September, and Lyndsay and I became comfortable without him for those few hours that he was gone. Because of the closeness and guardedness among us kids, it had been a concern whether Ronnie would allow us

---

[2] Pseudonyms have been used

to be separated from him while he was in school. It was the test that proved that we felt safe here.

Mrs. Graham took Lyndsay and me with her when she went shopping, and she bought us suckers and penny candies. We always saved some for Ronnie. In the evenings, we were allowed to sit on the couch with Mr. and Mrs. Graham and watch TV with them. We had a bedtime, and we did not argue about it. We were happy and contented children. We let our guard down.

Mr. and Mrs. Graham took us to church with them, and we got to go to Sunday School with all the other kids. It was a lot of fun. Lyndsay was too small to go to Sunday School, but they made an exception for her. When it got cold outside, the Grahams started to take us to the church on Saturdays. We started to learn Christmas songs, and we were given parts to recite at the concert.

We sang songs about a baby with no place to live and how angels stayed up all night to keep watch over him. I thought about how the baby should come and live with us; I wondered why the Grahams had not thought of that. I think the shepherds were like Mr. And Mrs. Graham because they came to see the baby, too. It filled my head with new possibilities and hope.

How exciting and special that time was. I had never had a Christmas tree in my house before, and the Grahams let us help decorate the tree. There was always a lot of happy laughter in the house.

Then came the night of the Christmas concert. We were all so excited and nervous. I sang the songs as hard as I could. I remembered every word of my part in the concert. So did Ronnie. And Lyndsay even had a line to say.

Mr. and Mrs. Graham were so proud of us. At the end of the concert, they gave us a big bag of candies and Christmas nuts and even a Christmas orange. I had never had a Christmas orange before.

When we got home from the concert that night, the Grahams asked us to sing a Christmas song for them, and when we were finished, they clapped their hands and cheered for us. Then they gave each of us a Christmas present to open. It was the first Christmas present I had ever gotten. I could hardly sleep that night. I wore my new Christmas slippers to bed on my hands. No one would be able to sneak in and steal them from me. I loved them so much. They were toasty warm and so pretty, with white fur around the top. Mine were pink, and Lyndsay got blue ones. They were the best treasure

Karrie and Lyndsay, Christmas 1959

I had ever had.

On Christmas morning, there were so many Christmas presents under the tree. There were presents for everyone. Lyndsay and I got great big fuzzy dolls with plastic faces and a bonnet-like brim around their faces. They were almost as big as me. Mine was pink, and Lyndsay's was blue.

Christmas day was so full of excitement and fun. Even Ronnie was happy. Lyndsay was Mr. Graham's favorite, and she could always climb up on his lap and lay her head on his shoulder whenever she wanted, and he never turned her away.

Mrs. Graham said I was too big to sit on her knee, but she was always happy when I sat beside her.

I had never seen so much food on the table as there was on the Christmas table. All us kids got to sit at the table with the Grahams. They taught us how to say grace. There was never more joy and peace in the world than there was that year when we spent Christmas at the Graham's house.

I think I loved Mr. and Mrs. Graham. I think they loved us. At least it was the closest thing that I could have called love.

But that too came to an end.

One day just after Christmas, Miss Benson and Mr. Webster knocked on the door. Again, we packed up our cardboard boxes of clothes and the new stuff we got for Christmas.

I did not know what I had done wrong, but I knew that it must have been really bad. This was the worst I had ever felt. I was so sorry that I had ruined it for Ronnie and Lyndsay.

We all cried: Mr. and Mrs. Graham, Ronnie, Lyndsay, and me. The Grahams walked us to the car and cried when they gave us all a big hug and kiss. They were standing at the side of the street, holding each other as they waved goodbye to us. I watched until we turned the corner, and they were gone.

I never saw them again, but I have never forgotten them. And tonight, I wept when I remembered them in my prayers. They were the brightest spot of my entire childhood.

Behind the Smile

We forgot to pack my new pink slippers with the white fur and the giant dolls!

Chapter 5 — A Litter of Unwanted Kittens

Once again, we were sitting in the back seat of a car and on the move. Three travelers were unwittingly embarking on a new life. Ronnie sat up as big and tall as he could with Lyndsay tucked under one arm, sucking her thumb, and me under his other arm. I wanted to be brave like Ronnie seemed to be, but inside I was just glad that Ronnie was with us. Secretly, I was glad that his arm was around me and that Lyndsay was on the other side of him because I did not want to be strong for anyone else but me. I felt dreadful and sad. I just wanted to cry but I couldn't. My stomach ached. My ears hurt. My heart was as broken as a four-year-old's heart can be.

We sat silently in the back seat, listening to the conversation in the front seat. I couldn't understand everything they were saying, but I knew that they were talking about us. They must have been taking us away because we were too much trouble for the Grahams.

"Did you bring the file with you?" asked Mr. Webster as he watched the road.

"Yes. Why?" responded Miss Benson.

"Oh, I'm just not sure how to get to the E farm. It's been awhile since I was out this way. And then I was only there the one time," Mr. Webster stated.

"So, you have met them then, eh?"

"Yeah. Just the once, though."

"What are they like?"

"Well, you know. Typical foster parent choice, I guess. Strong folk, but generous in nature, as I recall," he stated thoughtfully.

"Do they have any children of their own?"

Mr. Webster turned his head and frowned.

"You were supposed to read the file. Isn't that information in the file?" he questioned.

"Not that I recall seeing," she defensively said as she glanced out the side window. After a moment of silence between them, she asked again, "Well? Do they have any of their own children?"

"I don't recall," Mr. Webster answered impatiently after a long pause.

"You don't recall? I thought you were the worker that recommended the Es." Miss Benson squinted at the man.

"And so?" he defended in obvious challenge.

"Well, I just thought that if you were the worker that recommended this move that you would be more familiar with them."

"Look, Miss College Graduate. I don't think that I need to explain my recommendations to you. But if you must. Number one!"—he counted off on his fingers—"I have a heavy caseload on my desk, and I can't be expected to remember every little detail. Number two! The E farm is way out in the country, and you know how often these kids ran away in

Leduc. I believe that it would be best for everyone concerned for them"—he tipped his head toward the huddle in the back seat—"to be somewhat isolated, for their own good, I mean."

"Yeah, I'm sure," Miss Benson countered sarcastically. "And the best part that you missed is how hard it is to get qualified foster homes."

"Scoff at the system all you want, but it is true. It is difficult to find placements. Especially if we want to keep the kids together. We'll see how you feel about things in a year or two. If you last that long." The man looked straight ahead.

The woman looked out her side window. That conversation was over.

I looked over at Ronnie. His eyes were glazed, and he was staring straight ahead. I never quite knew what that meant when Ronnie's eyes got all empty looking. But I knew he wasn't really there anymore. Not really.

I turned my head and looked out the window. I could see the grey winter sky and occasionally the tops of trees that grew in the ditches along the country roads. I closed my eyes to the movie screen just behind my lids. *I could see him coming, his arms outstretched—"Who is my favoritist little princess in the whole world?"*

"I am Daddy. I am." I crawled up onto my daddy's knees and laid my head on his shoulder. I let my breath go out of me and felt my body relax. "I am Daddy—"

Behind the Smile

When the young social worker looked back at the children in the back seat, an uneasy feeling settled on her. The young boy in the middle was just staring straight ahead. His eyes were unfocused, glazed. The older of the two girls was whispering. Miss Benson could not make out the words, but the girl seemed to be chanting, repeating something over and over.

I wonder how much of our conversation the kids overheard, she thought. *Pathetic. Like a litter of unwanted kittens,* she sighed and looked back out her window.

Chapter 6 — Marlene

My grandmother was Sarah, a Métis woman born in Candle Lake, Saskatchewan, in 1895. Sarah moved to a small prairie farming community close to the Alberta border and married a farmer sometime before 1921.

To say that life was not easy on the family farm would be to understate the matter. The eldest daughter was born in 1913, and there was a new baby about every eighteen months.

The first two daughters were born before Sarah met Dickie Barnes, a proper English farmer, a good catch for a single Métis mother.

The family survived through the homestead years of the Canadian prairies, a time when no one had much but their farm and the love of their families.

The Barnes family survived the harsh realities of World War I, the great plague of the Spanish Flu of 1918, Black Thursday – the day the stock market crashed in October 1929.

Then two and a half months after the crash of 1929, Dickie died suddenly, leaving behind a pregnant wife and eight kids on a homestead that was mostly slough, willow bushes, and weeds.

Times were hard for Canadian prairie farmers. It would have been unimaginable for the Barnes family. Then, within four months of Dickie's death, on May 01, 1930, my mother, Marlene, was born.

It is easy to understand that Sarah and her brood of nine children struggled to make ends meet in a time in Canadian history when all the prairie farmers were struggling to survive. Sarah had a small farm and an admirable team of horses that were well used to working the land by Sarah and her young children.

The team was hitched up to a buckboard to carry the children to school in the town four miles away, five days a week; on weekends, everyone pitched in to work the farm according to their ability. They worked, or they starved.

Sarah was a Métis woman. The Métis had been swindled out of their land by the great Canadian real estate fraud called the Scrip. Many of the Métis people were pushed off their land and took to squatting on the road allowances – hence, the references to Métis as road allowance people. Sarah was a road allowance child.

Because health and education were tied to property taxes, and the road allowance people did not pay property taxes on the land they squatted on, their children were not eligible for education.

Sarah understood the importance of education for her children. It is unknown whether Sarah ever had any formal education, but if she did, it surely came from a residential school.

Education was the only thing Sarah knew would carry value for her children's futures; the only thing that she held hope in to make their lives different than the one she knew as a child.

One by one, Sarah's children matured, made it through school and left the farm with an education and a dream of a better life. The girls went on to successful marriages, at least in the aspect that none were ever divorced, and the boys all became men in service of their country as soldiers in the Canadian forces.

All of Sarah's children were fortified with a drive to survive and resilience that prevented them from drowning in poverty. They survived World War II and the Great Depression without the comfort and security of a male head of the household.

Not that there was no male presence on the Barnes' farm. There was no shortage of single men in the prairie farm community, and it was known and generally accepted that many of these men found female companionship at the Barnes' farm.

And so it was, that Marlene grew up. Sarah did whatever she needed to survive and for the survival of her children. It is this example that Marlene learned young – you did what you need to survive. All Marlene knew was dirt poor, hand to mouth poverty, and what she needed to do to survive was perhaps not acceptable in polite company, but was never outright discountenanced by the community either, as long as it did not involve the married men. All was well, as long as no one got hurt, and everyone was taken care of.

But Marlene did get hurt, unintentionally. How could she not? It was the only life she knew. It was the only image she had of fatherhood and what a woman needed to do to get by. Salt that with a large dose of anger and bitterness, and you have a young Marlene that was set upon the world.

In 1943 only Sarah and Marlene were left on the little homestead on the Saskatchewan prairie. With no man living on the farm, the community clucked their tongues and shook their heads sadly, when another Barnes baby boy was born. How sad, they whispered to each other. They incorrectly accepted the claim that Sarah had given birth to another child. The truth was even sadder and unimaginable. The new baby boy on the Barnes' farm was thirteen-year-old Marlene's firstborn.

Marlene grew up in a white farming community in a Métis family. She was different than the other kids at school. She was a half-breed.

Marlene was graced with the beauty afforded her from her Métis bloodline. She was also favored by enough of her father's white flesh to allow her to pass in whichever community she found favor in. She had the kind of beauty that men swooned over and just enough wildness to drive them crazy. The exact attributes that separated her from the women folk her entire life.

Marlene had a mean streak in her that may be easy to explain from her background. She had a ferocious temper and a mean mouth. Once a man got away from her, he never wanted to be reminded of her. More than one of her children's fathers were afraid to speak of the woman even decades later.

This was my mother. This may explain how any child of Marlene's was surely born into chaos. This may shed some light on what caused Marlene to be so crippled that she crippled everyone who touched her. This may give some satisfactory reason why she gathered men, fathers, children, and then inexplicably lost them all.

Marlene lost one baby to the grave and eight babies to the Department of Child Welfare: a provincial government agency that could care less about Marlene. But in their reckless endeavor to keep Marlene childless, they lost sight of the actual mandate of their department, and that was *The Best Interests of the Child*.

There have been volumes of books written that go into great detail regarding the topic of the legal depth of the term, *The Best Interests of the Child*, and the legal test by which the actions of government agencies are weighed. That topic is beyond the scope of this story, and better dealt with in another place to do it justice.

This is simply my story and not a thesis on the moral dilemma of the Child Welfare System.

Eight of Marlene's children suffered at her hands. Still, the same eight suffered greater tragedy and trauma at the hands of a heartless bureaucracy that sanctioned race-based initiatives based upon the notion of white benevolence – programs like Adopt Indian Métis (AIM) Program.

Métis birth mothers were often told that if they really loved their babies and wanted the best for them, they would give them up to people that wanted them and could provide better homes for them.

Although it goes against our nature as mothers who have carried our babies for nine months in our womb, Métis women were told it would be selfish not to.

Decades later, I was told, "I wish you could see the other side of this – the joy and the love that an adoptive parent has for a child they have chosen and waited so long for. It would be selfish for you to deny your baby this opportunity for a life with two loving parents – a mother and a father." It is preposterous that I could possibly believe them.

The government's Department of Child Welfare in Canada were willing to pay top dollar to non-indigenous foster homes. Still, they did nothing to ease the financial struggles of Aboriginals and Métis mothers so they could provide a safe environment for the nurture of their children. It is a deeply embarrassing time in Canadian history and a black eye to the Child Welfare systems of the provinces of Canada.

It is an era called the Sixties Scoop. Still, very few Canadians really understand the policy of wholesale Aboriginal child apprehensions. This is an issue that is yet unaddressed for the Métis people of Canada.

Marlene was stuck in a cycle of abuse and poverty and may be faulted for her shortcomings as a mother. However, the Department of Child Welfare in the provinces of Canada carries even greater fault.

Clearly, there were other options available to the government when it came to Marlene and her children. She had sisters and brothers, and the children had fathers. So, it seems clear to me that those avenues should have been investigated first *In the Best Interest of the Child*.

I understand, and it is arguable that Auntie Jean was not a viable solution. But I have met at least one uncle that was a sober and upstanding well-respected man in his community that grieved over the loss of his nieces and nephews. Why did the Department of Child Welfare never approach him?

The Department of Child Welfare did not understand or recognize the extended family system of the Métis people. Marlene had turned to her family for help. It was from the shelter of a family member that we were apprehended. And even with all the resources of the government of the province of Alberta at their disposal, it took the Department of Child Welfare about four years to convince a judge in the District Court in Edmonton, Alberta, that the granting of permanent wardship was necessary. One of the documents in my file showed that it was argued in court that it was in my best interest that I be made a permanent ward of the Department of Child Welfare in Alberta, so that I may be adopted by my foster parents.

When the court finally granted the order in 1963, my foster parents turned down the notion of adoption outright, with no discussion. I became a permanent ward of the Alberta Government.

Chapter 7 — Foster Home – Mrs. E

Some stories demand to be heard. This story has demanded of me, a voice for over sixty years. It has been denied a voice because of fear.

Coward. That's what I have been: a coward with no voice, living in fear, misplaced loyalties, shame, and guilt. And it is the single greatest regret of my life.

Although in spite of the manipulation, the grooming, the training to be compliant to the nth degree, somehow, I climbed out of that prison well of sewage. Against all odds, I cleaned myself off until no one could smell the stench of foster care on me. Today, it is only the E family and perhaps some of their closest friends who cling to some fantasy that I am filthy, and "they" are clean, and desperately hold that notion without evidence.

I became a strong, caring, loving woman, wife, and mother. I built fortresses around me to hide myself in, until through a deep enduring need to expunge the inner pain, I would raise the blinds slowly to those close to me. Often, my need to heal opened me to misplaced loyalties, wanting to trust – perhaps trusting too soon.

I was desperate for understanding and compassion. Invariably what I found was, love only stretches so far, and then it breaks. It only goes so deep, and then it ends.

I believed everyone has their limitations on what they can bear. Who has the strength and the love substantial enough to hear the depth of another's pain without judgement?

Or to believe all of it, not just part of it, because your experience does not allow you to comprehend it all.

As the pain unraveled and slithered out my gut, filling every single corner of the room under and over and on top, and it still comes. It fills the room until it evacuates even the oxygen – and still, it comes.

It has had sixty years to grow inside of me, every week and every moment of my life.

It has been hidden.

It has its own life.

It has been exposed, only to be hidden again.

And it has been fed – fed pain, shame, humiliation, terror, loneliness, rebellion, anger.

Sometimes I see parts of that creature, and I think it is one thing. I pray. I cry. I seek counsel. I read. I study. Hoping to understand, and above all to kill that dragon inside of me.

Then in a dream, I would identify another part of it. Oh! It is childhood abuse!

And the cycle of searching memories, self-inspection and introspection, research, reaching out – crush the dragon cycles again and again.

Each time the dragon would slither its way out my mouth, often terrifying me – certainly terrifying my audience.

But each time it would laugh at me, scoff at me, as it slithered back inside of me, whispering, "Wrong again! You do not know who I am, and my home is still inside of you." I was chained under the control of secrecy, as surely as if I were chained in a dungeon.

SECRECY! That's the dragon's name!

So today, at sixty-five years old, I hold my breath. I find the courage to replace the cowardice. And as I spill each word down on paper, I expose piece by piece, inch by inch, every bit of the dragon, until there is no lingering part of it in me. No tail, no foot, not a scale of it left so I can finally close the doors on it forever to live the remainder of my life in peace.

The first thing I realized in this process is: what is cowardice? Was I truly a coward? Or was that the voice of the dragon?

Yes, it was. When I would feel strength bubble up within my heart, its voice would extinguish my strength. Its voice would tell me: "You have never exposed them—you have never exposed anyone for what was done to you, so why do so now?" Suddenly I realized that the dragon inside of me was protecting my perpetrators all along.

I gained an inch of courage. The dragon lost an inch.

You have never talked. Who would ever believe you? They will leave you...everyone will leave you. They will laugh at you. They will curse you. They will call you a liar, a troublemaker. They will turn their backs on you. They will circle their wagons and join forces against you.

And just by saying that, I can laugh freely! Because why would I fear that? They already have! They have already circled their wagons, and I have been on the outside of their wagon train since before I was five years old.

What a revelation! What freedom that brings. Now the truth can be told.

I was brutally honest regarding my mother, Marlene and her faults and failures toward me. In clear conscience, I must be equally honest regarding the foster home, and the Alberta Department of Child Welfare.

***

It was New Year's Eve, 1959. It was the day that marked the end of that calendar year, and for me, it marked the end of what I believe my life should have been or could have been.

Late on that day, we were awakened in the back seat of the car. The two social workers from the Department of Child Welfare in Wetaskiwin, Alberta, were completing the transfer of three Métis children who had been apprehended in Leduc, Alberta, from the home of their aunt.

There was no fanfare and little introduction when we arrived at the white house with the blue trim on a farm about twenty miles from the nearest town. The social workers were simply doing their jobs, and Mr. and Mrs. E were simply there to open their door. It was all emotionless and sterile.

We were immediately sent to the basement that had two bedrooms. One, we were not allowed into. It was locked.

The basement was to be my home for as long as I lived in this house. We were allowed upstairs to cook and clean, and little else.

The room that was to be ours was uninviting, with a single bed along one wall and a double bed behind the door. Lyndsay, Ronnie and I had shared one bed since Marlene had left us. Suddenly, we were forbidden to share a bed. We were told with disgust dripping from their tongues, the immorality of brothers and sisters sleeping in the same bed.

The entire room was concrete, except the ceiling, which was open floor joists for the main floor. The walls were painted a pale green, and the floor was bare and cold concrete. It was austere and cold. And as we soon learned, so were the people who lived there.

From the precise first moment that I entered that house until the day that I left 162 months later, the atmosphere of that house and the relationships within it, with regard to me, never got any warmer or friendlier.

Perhaps the old-country German couple was not as old as they appeared to me from the point of view of a child, but clearly, they were ancient compared to Mama.

Mrs. E was a stout, tall woman with a non-descript, sour countenance. Her stern and expressionless face was infrequently broken by a thin mirthless grimace that represented a smile.

Her eyes were like chunks of grey coal that pierced through the lenses of her gold-rimmed glasses. A cold generous bosom pulled tight under her cotton farm blouse. She carried with her a vague smell of sweat – not pungent, just lingering.

A large flat rump followed by large thick legs ending in bare feet with knuckled toes and spider-webbed blood vessels in the hollow behind her ankles.

She had large hands capable of inflicting pain – and she did – often. They were red and rough patches of oozing eczema. Her rough flaking elbows scratched inside the cotton sleeves like they wanted out.

She had a thick waddle that wrinkled and swayed below her chin and disappeared behind the top button on her blouse.

All of her was held together with a spine as rigid as one-inch rebar.

Mrs. E was the boss, the warden – a force never to be reckoned with, and all who knew her knew not to attempt to push her. They treated her with the kind of healthy respect one would have for a polar bear.

And that is where her secret name came from. Ronnie said it first, and it stuck. The Polar Bear.

Mr. and Mrs. E were middle-class mixed farmers who lived on a half section of prime Alberta farmland. They had immigrated from Saskatchewan around the time of the Great

Depression. They married young, started a family of two boys and two girls, and completed the requirements of homestead to acquire their land. By the time the Es were in their late forties, they had established a thriving farm, their children were grown and had left the farm to embark on their own careers.

Frankly, that left the Es with a shortage of laborers on the farm. It is my belief that it was Ronnie who the Es were most interested in. He was to be their free labor. Even better, they were paid a regular paycheque every single month from an employer who had a secured line of credit. They would never again have to face a decrease in the paycheque. Sadly, this is not an uncommon theme among Métis and Aboriginal foster children.

1960 Lyndsay – age three, Ronnie – age nine, Karrie – age five

The problem in Mr. and Mr. E's plan was Ronnie turned out to be old enough to know too much and remember too much. He was strong-willed and emotionally twisted. He was too old to just be compliant. No amount of punishment or beatings could curb Ronnie. It just made him angrier.

The Es tried for about two years to break Ronnie's will. He became more and more dark and angry. He ran away and ran away. Every time he ran, the first thing the Es did was check to see if any of their guns were missing.

When Ronnie ran away, Es would double lock the doors, check all the windows and keep Lyndsay and me locked inside. They were afraid of Ronnie. They had beaten and abused him physically and emotionally until Ronnie was a rattlesnake ready to strike.

Even I knew that Ronnie was not right emotionally. He scared even me. But I still loved him with all my heart, and I needed his protection. He was like a father to me.

Friends and family of the E's were reluctant to visit the E's farm with their children. Ronnie would frighten the children with horrendous and shocking stories.

Ronnie would tell of his secret plans to drive around the country in his car that was *as dark as night and as light as day*, in other words, an invisible car. He was going to go around to all of E's family and kill them in their beds. He was going to kill the Es. And then he was going to kill Lyndsay and me, and then himself.

Elaborate stories for a nine-year-old child. Frightening insight into the shattered mind of a child.

And still, no social worker ever came and talked to any of us about what was going on, where this darkness was transpiring from.

One day a social worker drove into the yard just as the school bus dropped Ronnie and me at the gate. Lyndsay and I were rushed into a bedroom on the main floor of the house. Ronnie was ushered downstairs to his room, and a paper grocery bag of his belongings was thrown together. In minutes, they loaded him into the car and drove him away.

Ronnie was not allowed contact with us, or to speak to us; he was not allowed to wave to us or hug us; no parting words. Lyndsay and I were not told what was happening.

Mrs. E made Lyndsay and me sit down on the floor in the entryway and not even look out the window to see Ronnie being driven away. It was all very sterile, and cold. It was all very terrifying to two little girls left alone in a house that was worse than the boogeyman.

It remains one of the worst days of my life. Mrs. E forbid us to cry. She told us that it was a good thing that he was gone. She rewarded our silence and compliance by giving us a chocolate bar, or she plied us with it. Treats were far and few between at the E's. It was common for them to be used as weapons.

It was not the first time that I was demanded to jam my emotions down – I was already good at it. We were not allowed to cry. My emotions were bottled up tight inside of me, and it was unacceptable and forbidden to express them.

Then as salt in our wounds, as if we were invisible and deaf she pompously told all who had ears to hear how Lyndsay and I were so glad that Ronnie was gone. She told them that we did not even ask about him, that we did not cry, that we did not even care to wave goodbye to him. I was ashamed of my compliance. I had no resistance.

Lyndsay and I were devastated, and there was no one to comfort us or have compassion for us. The social workers never even looked at us, let alone speak to us about it: not before that day, to prepare us, not that day, as an act of kindness, and never after that day as an act of understanding or comfort. It was never discussed with us by anyone. We could not even discuss it between us – that would give it a voice and make it real – and the burden of that was just too great.

Ronnie had been the oldest of our abandoned litter[3]; he was the protector, and he was the parent figure – a phenomenon where, usually, the eldest child takes on the responsibilities as the parent. It is referred to as *parentification*. This is much similar to the role of Wendy in Peter Pan.

But Ronnie was now gone. That mantel fell on my shoulders. I was the one who had to remain vigilant and stalwart. I needed to fulfil the promise made to Ronnie, as I lay on my tummy under the rabbit hutch – take care of Lyndsay. I instantly felt the weight of that responsibility, and it remained for many years. I was now the parent of what remained of our litter.

We were wards of the Alberta Government. I knew that. I did not understand what that meant when I was small, not until much later.

---

[3] We were not legally abandoned. I have a copy of my Department of Child Welfare file, and in 2019 I had a career Social Worker read it. It is clear from my file that there were no legal grounds for apprehension, at least under the social workers policies and procedures today. If this event occurred today, we would never have been removed from Marlene's custody.

Through fourteen years as a ward of the government, I learned what it meant is that I belonged to the government. I was chattel. I came to understand it meant I was not a human child. I was something different. I breathed, I could bleed, I could feel pain, but I was not a human child.

Because if I were a human child, then I would have been worthy of love and care and nurture—someone, at some time when I belonged to the Government of Alberta, would have hugged me. But I was a ward. I was chattel. The Alberta government owned me.

Because I belonged to the government, they could do with me as they pleased. They were the ultimate authority. This was in the 1960s. Who would question the government?

I was placed in a foster home – in trust with strict religious people who were hard, cold and rigid, and often cruel.

Were they ever screened? I truly cannot say for sure. It would be my hope they were, and yet it would be better if they had never been screened.

Because if there was no screening, one could ask why not. But if there was screening, then I must say someone fell very short of their duty.

Mrs. E was, at best, mentally ill. She came from a family of much mental illness – a sister who committed suicide and a brother who ignited himself, both died after decades of mental instability and suffering. They lived reclusively and were carefully and continuously monitored by immediate family.

Both, in fleeting moments of lapse of supervision, seized their moments to tragically and violently end their lives.

Mrs. E was an extremely bitter, angry, malicious woman. Without a doubt, she was the most feared and hated woman in the community. She could never be pleased by anyone. She could not be made happy, and she sucked every morsel of happiness and joy out of everyone around her.

Even her grandchildren were afraid of her and learned what they would call, respect for her. It was not respect – it was fear.

Mrs. E never asked anything of anyone, she demanded. You never crossed her. You followed her commands to the letter and then went the next step and tried to appease her. And only those who were very good at doing that could escape her wrath if they were from within her inner sanctum.

I was not so fortunate. I did not fulfil the rules; they made me defensive, and then they made me angry, and then I became rebellious. I was fiercely protective of Lyndsay, but I was more afraid of Mrs. E.

In the fourteen years that I was a ward of the government, I heard Mrs. E laugh one single time with us. And in those fourteen years, I never received a single hug from her, and I would probably be correct in saying that she never praised me or encouraged me in any endeavor.

There was not a day that I was not afraid of her. I lived for fourteen years in a state of fear and hyper-vigilance. Mrs. E exuded just enough evil and blackness to hold me in fearful compliance. So, when I got away from the farm, and away from Mrs. E, I acted out in scandalous ways. I lived under such horrendous pressure that the instant the pressure came off, I would explode in outlandish behaviors.

Nearly fifty years have passed since I left the farm, and even to this day, I still have nightmares of Mrs. E chasing me down the country road in her new car…me running as hard as I can in the ditch in stark terror…her driving her shiny new car with her head out the window cackling like a witch and screaming, "I'll catch you."

In my dreams, she taunts me, threatens me.

To this day, in my dreams, I run as hard as I can. I am exhausted and ready to give up and allow myself to fall into the tall grass in the ditch. And just as I am ready to give up, terror overtakes me, and I know that if I stop, she will kill me.

Whether irrational or not, I lived for fourteen years in a home that I always feared I could be killed, at any time, and no one would care.

There was never any compassion or even any reasonable custodial care toward us. That first winter that we were at the Eses, they had some plumbing work done in the house. It was a frigidly, cold winter day.

Every day after breakfast, we had to go outside for at least an hour, so we were used to the cold weather, but this day it was extreme. Within a few minutes, I began to feel a bit panicky because it was just way too cold. Lyndsay was crying, and the tears were freezing on her cheeks and eyelashes. We huddled together in the corner of the house that afforded us shelter from the wind, and that felt better.

The plumbers went in and out of the house a few times, and when one went back into the house, he told Mrs. E that he thought it was too cold out there for the girls, and they were crying.

We were outside, directly under the window, so I heard the conversation. I was filled with terror.

Mrs. E came running outside and yelled at us. She created a big scene and production about us being out in the cold and not having enough sense to come in. She commanded us to stop crying and accused us of trying to make people feel sorry for us, and that we were too stupid to come in when it was cold and that we shouldn't have gone outside in the first place.

Like, holy hell! She forced us daily out in the cold, and then when someone called her on it, it was all our fault. It was always our fault. I grew up every day feeling like everything was always my fault, and moreover, I was told at every turn that it was my fault.

Our winter coats were too small for us, and the sleeves left about two to three inches of exposed skin at our wrists between the coat and our mittens. That exposed skin would freeze, then dry, and the skin would crack and bleed. That was our fault, too, because we were just too stupid to pull our sleeves down.

I remember one incident when Mrs. E was standing on the corner of the main street with several of her friends, and they were talking very disparagingly about Indians. Mrs. E pulled my pants down to show her friends what color an Indian's bum was. There was no limit to the depth or breadth of humiliation that Mrs. E would foist on us.

Her friends referred to us as E's little breed girls. That reference stuck and I was called that to my face by a neighbor of the E's when I was visiting in the town when I was in my fifties. Even at that time, some thirty years later, I could not speak up for myself, with a level of expectation of respect for my person or my heritage.

That same theme of calling us down to others carried over to every person that they knew. Es told all the neighbors, all their extended family, all their church friends. They told everyone repeatedly, at every turn and under every circumstance, how horrible we were and how hard she had it, how ungrateful we were, how lazy we were, how stupid we were, how dirty we were. There was never a kind word spoken to us or about us.

About a year or two after we arrived at the E's house, Mr. Webster, the social worker, dressed in his fine three-piece brown suit and tie, drove into the yard. Mrs. E told us to stay outside and play. We snuck up under the kitchen window and eavesdropped on the conversation. It was a trick I had learned from Ronnie. Mr. and Mrs. E spent an hour or two regaling the man with atrocious stories about Lyndsay and me.

Mrs. E was beside herself about how awful we were: how mouthy, how sullen, how angry, how dirty, broke everything on purpose, careless, had to keep everything locked away or we would steal it, pretend to be sick all the time, had to be told to do everything over and over. It just went on and on. I was about five or six years old. Even at that age, I understood what a liar was.

We were not allowed to back talk. We did not back talk. We got the back of their hand on our mouth; my earliest recollection of getting slapped in the face for speaking was when I was still four years old – within weeks of arriving at the E's.

Now I must ask – just how bad can a child possibly be? We were not ADHD or ADD or any such thing. We got on well when we went to school. Neighbors thought we were pleasant and well behaved. There must have been some merit in some of the things Mrs. E said about us, but much of it was either cut and dried lies or malicious fabrications. For the most part, we were compliant and quiet. We knew very well that punishment was swift and harsh. This was a household that did not make idle threats about punishment.

From an adult perspective many years later, I believe that Mr. and Mrs. E presented us in such bad light, that if, or more like it, when there was ever any trouble in the foster home, that no one would ever believe us.

Years later, when I received my Social Welfare file through the Freedom of Information Act, it was amusing to read Mr. Webster's notes of meetings with the Es, where he makes comments about Lyndsay and me.

"...are nice-looking and bright. They are dark-complexioned but could pass for French. They are very affectionate and get along well together and with other children."

That is a direct quote from my file from September 1959, before we went to the foster home at the Es. French? Evidently to be Métis was unacceptable.

***

Extracted portions of my file notes:

Dec 29, 1959 – The children were moved to the home of Mrs. E on this date.

Feb 10, 1960 – have adapted themselves to this home very well, and Mrs. E is very happy with them. The girls are very appealing in order to apply for permanent wardship and thus pave the way for adoption.

Jun 02, 1960 – are very happy here, and Mrs. E is very much in love with them. They are kept spotlessly clean and are normal contented little girls. Have appeared to have forgotten their mother's existence, but there is still a deep-rooted fear of being moved.

October 1960 – excellent placement. Both girls have responded well to it. Both the girls have now begun to speak of their sister. Everything is under control here.

Mar 4, 1963 – was visited at the E home this date. Is a happy, healthy child. There are no problems.

Oct 23, 1963 – they are both happy and healthy and making good progress in school. There are no problems. Mr. and Mrs. E are extremely fond of these two little girls and give them a great deal of affection.

Nov 10, 1964 – very happy. Receiving excellent care. Making excellent progress. No problems.

May 10, 1965 – making excellent progress and are very happy here. The Es are very fond of the girls and are providing them with much needed love and security. The girls are developing as normal little girls and are making fairly good progress in school.

May 9, 1968 – have been approached concerning adoption but feel they would not like to proceed on this vein.

***

It is impossible for me to reconcile the file notes that I read. The seemingly touching comments regarding the E's sentiments toward us is – bewildering to me. Where did that come from? Social workers never spoke to us kids, and they never viewed interactions between us and the Es.

Even when I eavesdropped on a meeting between the Es and Mr. Webster of the Department of Social Services, my social worker whom I had never spoken to, a man who never said anything more to me than, "Hi," when he walked to the house, I could do nothing but shake my head in disbelief.

What I see is a social worker that was attempting to pave the way through a paper trail, for an argument in court for permanent wardship. I believe that it was the department of Child Welfare's hope that they would gain permanent wardship, and they would then adopt us. We would then be off their caseload. But Es did not want any part of adopting us, as is clear in the May 1968 file entry.

I already knew that. It had been discussed at family functions as if we were invisible and deaf and with their friends.

It is astonishing to me that none of the negative rantings from Mr. and Mrs. E in the conversations I eavesdropped on appears anywhere in my file. Why not?

If I had not overheard the conversation mentioned here above, I might have read my file and wondered. I just cannot fathom this.

And it is also astonishing to me that the Department of Social Services reported in 1959 that the living conditions at Auntie Jean's were 'adequate.' Still, they made application to the District Court in Edmonton for permanent wardship and extinguishment of Marlene's parental rights on the grounds of 'neglect.'

I think it is also notable that Mr. Webster, the social worker on my case from the day we were apprehended through the court cases which lasted from 1959 – 1964 when we were made permanent wards, was removed as our social worker right after.

I am left-handed and nearly ambidextrous. Mrs. E insisted that I eat with my right hand. For me, the spoon felt equally comfortable in either hand, and I could not remember which hand was my right hand. I was afraid of Mrs. E and terrified of her wrath, so I tried every mealtime to do it right.

One night, when I was about six years old, Mrs. E, like a flash, reached across the table and whacked me on the top of my hand with a sharp knife. It was not a usual utensil to be on the table. She had specifically brought it to the table that evening for that purpose. The knife cut into the top of my hand. She yelled at me to use my right hand. My left hand was bleeding all over my leg throughout the rest of the meal. Mrs. E showed no concern for me and no remorse for her actions.

My hand healed, but the knife cut left a scar. After that, before I ever picked up a utensil at the meal table, I looked for the scar on my 'no-no' hand, so I knew to use the other one.

When I got out on my own, some of the E family members told me that they were disgusted with the Es and how they treated us. Still, I can't help wondering what was wrong with people when they knew what was going on and did nothing?

We were not part of the family. We lived there for fourteen years. Their grandsons were similar to our age. But not one single Christmas or Easter or Thanksgiving were we ever allowed to sit at the table for the celebration dinner. Lyndsay and I sat out in the entryway of the house, on the floor with an old coffee table for a table. We never even sat in the same room.

On Christmas day, Lyndsay and I would have our chores to do in the kitchen to prepare the Christmas dinner. The rest of them – everyone else – would go in the living room and open gifts. We were not allowed in the room until everyone else was finished, and the dinner was ready to be put on the table. There was never anyone to witness any joy or excitement we felt for our gifts.

There was always a family photo on top of the fridge or on a wall, and it was renewed every year or so. Lyndsay and I were never included in a family photo. In fact, there was never a single picture of either of us placed anywhere in the house. A child who is wholly a part of a family and has a sense of belonging may not even notice the absence of a photograph of themselves anywhere in the house. I did notice – I did not belong – not even a facade of belonging.

In September, when we went back to school, we would be issued a materials and supply list from the school. Evidently, it was very important that everything that would be needed for the year was on that list. Mrs. E told the school every year that she was only allowed a requisition once a year. The letter that came from the Welfare Department stated that the form must be made out in duplicate.

Mrs. E convinced the department store where she bought our school supplies from that what it meant was that they needed to duplicate the order. I was present when the owner, Mrs. S questioned the matter with Mrs. E, but what would the owner of a store, care if the government was being swindled by a few dollars? It was not her responsibility to keep Mrs. E honest, so she filled both of the supply lists in double quantities.

All the school supplies went into a closet in the guest bedroom, and Lyndsay and I had to prove the need for more paper or other supplies by showing how much we had used. Items such as crayons were reused year after year, even though two new sets were supplied every year, for each of us. She doled the supplies out like bread in a Nazi concentration camp. Predictably, all the extra school supplies were sent over to her grandsons.

In Junior High School, it was the rules of the school that every student needed to have separate running shoes for the gym or go barefoot.

Mrs. E went to Edmonton, shopped at the Army and Navy, and came home with four pairs of boys running shoes. All four pairs went over to her grandsons.

Later that month, Lyndsay and I opened the letter that Mrs. E had prepared for the welfare and was on the counter awaiting mail day and we read it.

It was Mrs. E's requisition sent to the welfare, requesting reimbursement for out-of-pocket expenses for four pairs of running shoes. The explanation was the school required us to have a separate pair of runners to wear in the gym.

Lyndsay and I were told to wear our runners from last year to school and to go barefoot in gym class. I was the only student in my grade that was barefoot in the gym, so after a few weeks, the teacher told me I could wear my runners in the gym.

Mrs. E was always aloof and cold toward Lyndsay and me. About the only thing I ever remember her actually talking to us about was Marlene. She told me from the time I was perhaps six or seven years old that our mother was a whore. I didn't even know what a whore was. By the time I came to understand what the word had meant, I had been told that I was just like Marlene until the line of personal self-image was completely blurred for me. Who tells a six-year-old child that they are a whore?

I sprained my ankle when I was in grade five, and Mrs. E insisted that I was faking it to get out of doing chores, or else to get attention. Her story changed depending on what the circumstances dictated. This was Mrs. E's common response to any ailment, disease, condition, or physical damage when it came to me.

There was something very wrong with my ankle. The pain was so intense I was sick to my stomach, sweating, and had a headache. Mrs. E told me to get dressed and get to school.

I went to school, but I was feverish and passing out in class, so my teacher sent me to the sick room. The first course of action Mrs. U, who was a neighbor friend of Mrs. E and a teacher at the school, was called to look at me. She suggested that the principal be involved in the matter. Mrs. U knew Mrs. E well. She was not going to be involved in an issue involving the breed kid. Mrs. U appeared to be a confident, self-assured and educated woman, but she was not going to risk Mrs. E's wrath. And again, here was a woman that knew what was going on in that foster home, and she never reported it to the Department of Child Welfare. She did nothing.

The principal came to the sick room to check on me. There were phone calls placed to the Es, but they could not contact them. For some reason, the E's younger son was contacted, and he suggested that if the school could not contact the Es that they should go ahead and do what they felt was appropriate. Shortly thereafter, the principal drove me down to the medical center for a doctor to examine me.

The doctor admitted me to the hospital, and within a couple of days, surgery was performed. I spent weeks in the hospital.

Mrs. E was a tyrant. Initially, she was incensed and accused me of playing it up at school to get out of doing my chores at home or to get attention. Then she accused me of trying to get her into trouble by lying about how bad my ankle was injured.

Mrs. E carried on and on and berated me for weeks about what a horrible predicament I caused her. Finally, after being in the hospital for about five weeks, Mrs. E stormed into the hospital and accused the doctor of medical misconduct.

It was all such a mystery and embarrassment to me because of all the uproar and gossiping in the hospital until I got a copy of my Department of Child Welfare file through the Freedom of Information Act in 1994. Suddenly, a lot of things became clear to me.

It all became quite clear to me what the real problem was when I read in my social welfare file, that Mrs. E was temporarily removed as my guardian. The guardianship had been given to the hospital. I had not been in the foster home for a one-month period of time. The actual issue was money. They did not get paid for me that month.

Once again, I cannot understand why the people around this situation who knew what was going on did not stand up for me. Surely someone at the hospital or the school would have spoken up?

When the Department of Child Welfare was already involved in the guardianship issue over a breach jurisdiction due to lapse of time, why was there no investigation conducted?

When Mrs. E stormed into the hospital and raved at the hospital staff, why was she never investigated?

When the school could not locate Mr. or Mrs. E to get permission to take me to the doctor, why was there no investigation?

When I had been sent to school by the foster parents, and the school realized how bad my health was in this instance, why was there never an investigation?

I might be speculating here, but if Mr. and Mrs. E were Aboriginal people, and their own children were being treated in the manner we were, it is my firm belief that their children would have been removed, and likely with very little investigation. If the Department of Child Welfare was so concerned about the care and welfare of children, they should have started in the homes that they placed foster kids.

Further, I cannot understand where the fiduciary *duty of care* that the Alberta Government had, in my case, was. I went into foster care when I was four years old, and the first time that I spoke to a social worker was when I was fifteen or sixteen years old and ran away from the foster home.

I ran away on a Friday and caught a Greyhound bus to Calgary. Somehow, I had found out that Marlene lived in Calgary and possibly Ronnie as well. I got the idea in my head that I would find my mom and my brother and that I would get my whole family back together. This was not a sudden thought. I had entertained thoughts and plans of running away nearly every single day for years. I was just scared that Lyndsay and I would be separated. A thought I could not bear. But if I could find Marlene and get our family back together, then Lyndsay would finally be safe.

I was unsuccessful in my attempt and ended up turning myself into the RCMP in Calgary. I told them I was a runaway foster kid, and my social worker was in Wetaskiwin. The RCMP officers did not even believe me. I had not even been reported as missing. One of the responsibilities of a foster parent is to report a missing ward immediately.

The RCMP finally got ahold of my social worker who called the Es and found out I had been gone for a week already. I got taken to juvenile detention, and two days later, Mr. and Mrs. E came to Calgary and picked me up.

When the detention center workers came and got me out of the class I was in and told me my mom was there to get me; I was so excited.

Then suddenly, I was filled with terror, and I asked whether it was my mom or my foster mom. She left to find out, and when she returned, she told me it was my foster mom. I lost it so totally. I was in a state of absolute terror. I was certain that if they made me go with the Es that they would take me out to the country and murder me. I was in panicked terror. I had no choice. I resigned myself that I could be leaving the Detention Center to my death.

Once again, why was this event never investigated?

When I got back to school, I got a visit from my social worker. It was the very first time since I was put into foster care, about twelve years, that a social worker spoke to me and asked me how I was doing and how I felt.

In very veiled terms, I told him that I hated it. I could not speak in specifics of the horrors. I could not tell him about the beatings, the constant vigilance, the abuses, and their nature. I had no voice. I was not allowed to speak. Everything was packed in secrecy. I understood the punishment to Lyndsay and me. I could not do it.

I hated the foster home. I told him I did not want to be there anymore. He told me he would come out to the farm that night, but I had to tell him in front of Mr. and Mrs. E that I did not want to be there anymore.

There was no guarantee that Lyndsay would be taken with me, and there was certainly no guarantee that I would be leaving the house that night. I could not do it.

I was scared to death of these people. I sincerely thought that if I spoke up and then either of us or both of us were left in the E home, that they would kill us. So deep was my fear of them.

So, at that point, I felt that I had let myself down, and I was now the blame for my predicament. I decided I only had about a year and a half left, that I just had to hunker down and do my time. That's what I did.

I was a troubled teenager; there is no doubt. I know that there were educated people around Lyndsay and me. There was always a social worker assigned to our files. There were teachers and guidance counsellors. I cannot understand how no one looked at the situation of bizarre behaviour and questioned it, even a little. I shake my head in utter disbelief that no one saw that there was an underlying corruption causing the acting out. So thorough was the coverup, and façade, I suppose.

It brings to mind a situation regarding a neighbor that took up foster parenting. One of the foster girls jumped out of the upstairs bedroom window in the dark hours of the evening. Of course, no one believed the foster kid when she claimed she did so because the foster father was again entering her room after everyone else was asleep. Why would anyone believe that after the foster parents had told the entire neighborhood that she was an exceptionally troubled kid? *Troubled or not, who just jumps out their second-story bedroom window in the dead of night, I wonder as an adult looking back.*

One day shortly after I turned eighteen, Lyndsay and I arrived home from school, and the E's youngest son was there. Very surprising. We stood in the kitchen, listening to the conversation.

Their son stated that he and the E's youngest daughter had concerns about the way that we girls were being spoken to.

The conversation was a few short minutes, and Mr. and Mrs. E began shouting and crying. Mr. E stomped off to their bedroom, roaring that their son was, "Nothing but a goddamn social worker." He slammed the bedroom door so hard the house shook.

Their son just quietly left the house and drove away. That began a new treatment for Lyndsay and me. We were first of all interrogated regarding whether we had tattled to their kids, that we lied to their kids, and got them in trouble. Once they got phone calls from their kids and were convinced that Lyndsay and I had nothing to do with the incident, Mr. and Mrs. E withdrew everything from us.

It was a miserable hostile silence. They said nothing to us. Not one single word for weeks. They no longer came to our room to wake us in the morning; if we missed the school bus, we walked the twenty miles to school – that had always been the rule. They were sullen at best, and at worst, they seethed.

None of that scenario was in any way my or Lyndsay's fault, but we paid the price for it, and those whose fault it was did not take responsibility for their actions or tried in any way to relieve the troubles they created for us. Why could they not have just stayed out of it for four or five months longer? I would have been gone. After all, they had already looked on silently for fourteen years, what was another four months to them?

My eighteenth birthday was in February, and I was scheduled to graduate in June. Because I turned eighteen, I was no longer a legal ward of the Alberta Government. This created a fiscal dilemma for Mr. and Mrs. E and for the Department of Child Welfare. I was instructed to write a letter to the Department of Social Welfare requesting that they continue my wardship until I graduated high school in June. The request was granted, and Mr. and Mrs. E continued to collect their paycheque until the end of August 1973, two months after I was finished high school, and two months after I was gone from Es.

On my last day of high school, I came home on the school bus, and Mrs. E met me in the kitchen.

She made a big production out of slowly dusting off her hands, and she very slowly said, "I've–done–my–duty–you are now on your own."

And with that, she handed me a paper grocery bag with a couple of tops and some underwear and another bag with a pot, a plate, a coffee mug, a butter knife, and a spoon. I had – not one penny in my pocket.

I never had much for clothes or belongings anyway, but I was not allowed to take my belongings with me. When you are a foster child, nothing belongs to you. Ronnie left with next to nothing, as did I.

Mrs. E drove me into town and dropped me off at the sidewalk in front of a house that I had never seen before. She told me that was where I lived now; that she paid for one month of room and board and that I was to report to a supervisor at a restaurant the next morning about a job. I got out of the car, and she drove away.

I never saw Mr. E that day. He never said goodbye or wished me well. It meant nothing to me either way. I was never part of that family, and I was now on my own. And I was finally free of the hell I had lived for fourteen years.

If there were ever any misgivings about whether I was a part of that family, Mr. and Mrs. E's actions on that last day cleared up every doubt.

The place that I was supposed to live in was with an old lady who was a hoarder. The house was filthy and crammed full of junk from wall to wall and floor to ceiling. She showed me to my room, which had nothing more than a bed with a sheet and blanket. The whole house wreaked. It was so totally disgusting.

I might have slept there once. I could not stand it. I reported to work the next morning, and I was totally not well received. It was obvious that the supervisor was going to teach me some lessons in life. I could not understand the hostility. It is almost like it was Mrs. E's final revenge on me—the most despicable living conditions and a job with people who were already influenced.

I think the worst part of the whole affair was how unprepared I was for life on my own. I knew nothing except to follow orders.

I had no voice. I was never allowed to speak my mind about anything. I was not allowed to ask questions or to question things. I was not allowed to stand up for myself or Lyndsay. I was not even allowed to make simple decisions for myself, what to wear, when to bath, how to wear my hair.

I had never owned a toothbrush.

I had never been to a grocery store. I didn't even know what a paycheque was or what to do with it. I asked the girls at work what I do with the cheque, and they gaped at me and frostily told me to take it to the bank. I had never been to a bank. I didn't even know where the bank was.

I knew how to work, and I knew how to take orders and keep my mouth shut.

I had never chosen a haircut. Mrs. E just took me to a neighbor girl that pretty much bowl cut my hair. Mrs. E said it was a pixie cut.

I went from very strict, rigid parameters and rules to none. And I had no idea what to do. I was lost and scared.

Speaking ill of Lyndsay and me was a systematic devaluation and demoralization of us perpetrated by the very people who were paid by the Department of Child Welfare, that undertook an obligation to care for us. The Department of Child Welfare breached its duty to care for us.

They did not adequately follow up on our placement as it regarded Lyndsay and me. How is it that Lyndsay and I were the clients, and yet the social workers never once spoke to either of us until about 1971. And even when they did know of major breaches of custodial care, according to their own records, they failed to protect us.

When I was nearing the end of my wardship and aging out, they did absolutely nothing to ascertain whether I was prepared or whether there were any plans in place for me.

It has been thrown in my face repeatedly, how well all the E's children have done in their lives, and the grand successes of their grandchildren are, compared to my life. But there is no recognition that all their family was nurtured, groomed for further education, and encouraged in their endeavors. They had guidance and counsel, and financial support.

But Lyndsay and I were clearly not part of their family, and the entirety of that process was missing. I was never even asked the simple question, "What do you want to be when you grow up?" Furthermore, if I had ever been asked that question, how would I ever know? I had never been allowed to make a decision in my life, how could I conceive of that question?

And if there is nothing else in my testimony or in my file that proves the complete lack of parental involvement or care and concern, or whether I was in any way a member of the E family, much less whether there was any bounty of love anywhere in that relationship, it is in what happened in the last few months before I aged out and left to find my own life. That was not love.

It came as no surprise to me when not one member of the E family attempted to call me or keep in touch with me.

I had no friends to rely on. All the kids I knew had long ago stretched their legs and had lives of their own established. They had jobs, families, boyfriends, all things that I was not allowed to have. I did not fit in with anyone.

I found friendship with the kids from school that I knew smoked pot and partied. From there, I learned to survive. I hardly remember anything about my life for the next seven years.

In those seven years, I got married, had a baby, got divorced. That all took one year. Then I was a single mom trying to survive, if not for me, then for my baby.

Today, it saddens me that I spent fourteen foundational years in the home of Mr. and Mrs. E, and from the perspective of my slowly progressing healing and a place of quiet peace in my life, that I am still unable to recognize or sense any maternal or paternal conduct. I still see no love, or tenderness, or parental concern or guidance.

I still have a hard time standing up for myself or speaking up for myself. I was never allowed a voice in my childhood. I did not know how to speak up for myself; that was a skill that was foreign to me. I often experienced verbal paralysis from fear; when a person of authority spoke to me, I could not say a word in defense or explanation. Just the sound of disapproval or demand or command in another's voice, and I became pitifully mute to defend myself. Like a tsunami, I was swept out of my family – snatched away – taken – then separated from Ronnie. For fourteen years, the undercurrents of the foster care process crushed me to the floor of the sea and dragged me across the coral reefs and jagged rocks and pressed me under the surface without breath or voice. At eighteen years old, in July 1973, the crashing waves vomited me out on a desolate, barren beach with nothing. For the following nine years, I struggled with substance abuse and toxic relationships, dragging my baby along with me.

Today, I am still left with the picture of an emotional desert, except for the outcroppings of anger and contempt that was the prevailing panorama.

I remember the day that I stood at my daughter's kitchen sink, and a poignant thought crossed my mind. I was choked with emotion and bewilderment. I watched my grandson playing on the floor. This beautiful four-year-old child was loved so deeply.

I whispered to my daughter, "Look at him. Can you imagine if something happened to you, and he ended up living with someone else, and they never learned to love him—ever?"

My heart was shattered. It was one more merciful revelation to me of an area that so desperately required healing—is the beginning of another process.

Often, the sheer number of hurtful and destructive situations was overwhelming. I felt crippled. I grieved and felt like I was so broken I could never be healed.

Chapter 8 — Mr. E

Mr. E was about a half a head shorter than Mrs. E. He was a stout, squatty, heavyset man and rather barrel-chested. He sported a thickened middle, tied in with a worn two-inch leather belt. He had an older replica of that belt that had lost its buckle that was used liberally to keep the wayward breed kids in line.

Mr. E had chiselled features, eyes that were piercing like an eagle that overlooked a short-bridged nose that was thick, complete with nostrils filled and overflowing with hair. Bushy eyebrows topped those piercing eyes.

Mr. E had a thin-lipped smile that he showed with relative frequency that could be mistaken for warmth and appealing kindness, but for the darting, shifting look of his eagle-like grey eyes.

His sun-beaten-leather face stood on top of a thick neck that ended with a tuft of grey chest hair that escaped the top of his medium green work shirt. In the middle of his neck sat an Adam's apple that bobbed up and down, like the heads of gophers at the entrances of their holes in the spring.

Similar to his eyebrows and nose hair, his over-long ear lobes had tufts of bristly hair escaping the earholes.

He had long strands of always greasy greying hair combed over his balding head, leaving a tufted ridge of hair growing around the circumference of his head.

Years of hard work on the homestead had created iron muscled arms, as big around as my head. His rough paws were completed with thickened fingers like overstuffed breakfast sausages.

What stood out the most with Mr. E, was his respiration – hard, like it was being forced from his lungs, vaguely rasping, and puffing like a steam engine. He would have been fun to play hide and seek with – you could hear his breathing long before you saw him. But to play with the foster kids, the breed kids, was as foreign and taboo as cursing and laughter or tarried obedience.

The number one rule was to obey – to the letter and immediately. Imagination and initiative were forbidden.

Outside of that, the most important rule was secrecy. This rule was never written down anywhere, and it did not have to be reinforced by lectures. It was crystal clear. Just the terror I felt inside at the prospect of breaking this rule, kept my mouth clamped shut for decades.

Up until this year, I have had recurring nightmares several times a year. The theme always remains the same in these dreams, but the scene varies.

One time I will dream I am sitting at my desk at work and just as my boss walks in the room, I realize I am not sitting on my desk chair, but on a five-gallon bucket, a slop pail, so to speak – a toilet of sorts, that humiliatingly reeks of shit, and I, embarrassed, try to shuffle my skirt, so it drapes around the bucket. I try to pretend it is not a shit bucket. I try to pretend that I do not know that I am sitting on a shit bucket, but the stench of shit permeates the room, and I know everyone can smell it. But if I can just pretend, if I can just ignore it, then maybe no one else will notice. But of course, that just isn't true, and I know that everyone can smell it and knows I am shitting right there.

In another dream, the scene may change to where I am standing at the alter on my wedding day like everyone else, and then I am no longer standing, but sitting on a shit bucket, and I try to adjust my wedding dress so no one will know. But the reek of shit permeates, and I know it is not a secret, and everyone is looking at me with disgust, and I feel intense shame and humiliation.

In every dream – no matter what the scene, I try so hard to hide the reality of the scene, but the smell always alerts everyone around that I am sitting on a shit bucket and am shitting right there in front of everyone.

The E's farmhouse had modern bathroom facilities, a spacious bathroom off the kitchen, and between the two bedrooms on the main floor of the house. As a child, I was never allowed to use the indoor plumbing.

There was an outhouse behind the large farm garage about 250 feet from the house. That was for my use (and my siblings' use) only. No guests were ever expected to use the outhouse, nor were Mr. and Mrs. E's children and grandchildren. Whether we had guests, and no matter what our state of health was, we were never allowed to use the indoor toilet.

I can recall many times being extremely sick, with the flu and graced with massive bouts of diarrhea and having to get up repeatedly in the middle of the night, in the midst of Alberta prairie blizzards in the dead of winter, get dressed in boots, hat, farm chore coats and trudge through driving freezing snow to sit on a frozen outhouse seat to do my business. Insult to that injury was we were never allowed to have store-bought rolled toilet paper. We used crumpled up newspaper, and if we were lucky, the tissue wrappings of cased peaches and pears.

You might be thinking, so what? Tons of people used outhouses in the 60s, but I would say, fair is fair. If the whole family out of necessity used the outhouse, that is one thing, but when it was only my sister and me – only the foster kids, clearly, not family, that were relegated to face the elements and the outhouse then I reckon that is not fair. And even if I could draw a distinction between adults and kids, I cannot tolerate any argument that being forced in the middle of winter and the dead of night, in sickness outside to the outhouse to be deemed as anything other than intentional cruelty.

Outside of the logistical factors regarding the outhouse, I hated it because it meant very carefully searching the farm to locate where Mr. E was at – then estimating how much time I would need to sneak to the toilet and complete my duties before he could get to the outhouse. It was constant vigilance or holding myself as long as it took until I could make the run to the outhouse without Mr. E scooting up to the outhouse to watch through the knotholes. It was excruciatingly humiliating and a scenario that has plagued me for over sixty years.

And the truth of the matter was, often enough, I could hear his steam engine deep breathing before I could ever see his eyeball in a knothole.

The sound of his heavy chested, deep breathing was also a sound that, for many reasons, brought fear and even terror to my heart. My sister and I lived in the basement, where we shared a lumpy double bed that sagged in the center, in one room.

A wall separated our bedroom from the furnace room. There was an open hole in the base of the wall – an air vent without a cover on it. Often in the evenings, as my sister and I were getting ready for bed, we would suddenly hear his deep raspy breathing, like a bull, on the other side of the wall. He would be down on his knees, bent right over with his head at the floor level, watching us. When I realized he was there, it would cause a shock of fear and panic to rip through me. If we were in the midst of getting changed into our pajamas, we would flee into our closet to get dressed.

For thirty plus years and through two marriages, I had problems with modesty and the ability to undress in my husband's presence. I would go into the bathroom and lock the door or change in the closet.

We would place objects in front of the hole in the wall but would find the object mysteriously moved when we came home from school, so it was just easier to change in the closet. It was an obvious sign that we had no reasonable expectation of privacy.

We were powerless to complain. We were not allowed to express our feelings on any matter. We had been conditioned since we were three and four years old that we were not allowed to tell or complain, or even ask questions. We had no voice. We were not allowed to express any emotions, and we were not allowed to express our preferences regarding any matter.

We answered questions that were asked with the correct answers as we were conditioned to respond. We knew what the correct answers were, and we knew that the punishment would be extreme if we spoke out of line.

We were so fearful of any act of rebellion or resistance that if the box or object was moved, we were unable to make a stand and move it back.

How can I express how deeply conditioned and controlled that we were that it was terrifying to commit an outright act of rebellion to protect our pre and pubescent dignity and modesty? It was just easier to hide in the closet.

When Mrs. E would be away from the farm, Mr. E. began forcing me to read filthy jokes, some of them so horrendous that I actually attempted to push them away rather than finish them. This was a stage in his grooming process. Little by little, he broke down my barriers of resistance.

I remember Mr. coming home from town on a Wednesday when I was perhaps ten years old. Mr. E caught me in the pump house and held me tight in a bearhug. He seemed distraught with emotion.

He said, "What have you been up to?"

I had no idea what he was getting at.

He said, "Who have you been letting screw you?"

I was so instantly sick inside and mortified. I had never been kissed! I did not even have a secret crush. Sex was not even in my mind yet. He said someone wrote on the men's bathroom wall in the Chinese restaurant in town "For a good time, call Karrie." And my phone number.

Oh, my God! I am sick just writing this fifty-five years later! I was crushed and demoralized back then, and it was something that seared my brain and sickened me for years.

I fretted and worried about that for months. I was wounded and suspicious and disgusted. I could not get over it. I couldn't sleep – I laid awake at night, fretting about it and trying to work it out.

I thought, is *it possible that Mr. E lied?* But I couldn't figure out why he would tell such an atrocious lie. But nothing else made any sense. I continued to scrutinize every boy's face at school, and every word spoken to me for hidden meaning.

As an adult, and looking back on that incident, I am convinced that there was no truth to the story - it was just part of his grooming process.

Mr. and Mrs. E never frequented the Chinese restaurant in town. It was beneath them. At the age of ten, I was so backward and uncool, there is not one young fellow in the entire region that would have even known I was alive, let alone have the audacity to write such a thing on the bathroom wall about me.

The final "tell" for me remains, he never told Mrs. E. If it had been the truth, it would have been worthy of a few months of tirades, insults, shaming, and of course, new fodder for gossip with the neighbors and family about the wretched little breed girl.

I have considered whether I would have been able to make a stand somewhere along the way if it had not been for Lyndsay. It was always harder for me to watch Lyndsay being beaten or abused that it was for me to take the punishment.

By the time Lyndsay was seven years old, she had already figured out that I would take the rap for her and confess to her misdeeds to protect her.

Lyndsay would tattle on me for any infraction of the rules that she witnessed, and I would be punished. Little by little, there was a wedge driven between Lyndsay and me.

Lyndsay's defense mechanism was to play the part of the sweet little angel; the baby and baby talk her way through situations. She often acted inappropriately child-like, including feigning physical inabilities and using baby talk to get around the Es. She feigned naivety and widened her big brown doe eyes - it worked for her then and does so today. It is disconcerting, to me, to hear a sixty-something woman change her voice to that of a baby and talk baby-talk when she speaks of emotional or sensitive matters.

I, on the other hand, would correctly be considered hyper-vigilant, furtive, secretive, moody, and tougher. I was Lyndsay's shelter and protector.

One day, Lyndsay missed the school bus, and her friend's mother drove her home. Mrs. B begged Mr. and Mrs. E not to punish Lyndsay. I think that was what sent them over the wall. Someone tried to interfere; that means Lyndsay must have said something to make the Es look bad.

They lost control so completely, and savagely beat Lyndsay. They whipped her on the back and legs and butt until the skin broke and bled, and they still did not stop. Lyndsay screamed and cried, and still, it went on until Lyndsay was silent.

They tag-teamed the beating. When one wore out, the other would take over. They yelled insults and threats until they were breathless.

So out of control they were, that I thought for sure they were going to kill her, and when Lyndsay went silent, I thought they had. Even after Lyndsay went silent, they continued. To this day, it is the most savage thing I have ever witnessed.

I was terrorized. I screamed and begged them to stop. Then they turned on me. I ran downstairs, crying and screaming for them to stop.

In the E's household, we were not allowed to swear. I ran back up the stairs and again was stopped by Mr. E. I started to scream, "Fuck off, fuck off—STOP!"

They turned on me and threatened to start on me too. I sobbed, "You are going to kill her. Please, stop." I stumbled back downstairs.

When it finally ended, and Lyndsay came downstairs, there was fire and hatred in her eyes. I think she blamed me for not protecting her. She would not speak to me. She laid down on the bed on her stomach and didn't move or speak until she had to do her chores.

I was ashamed of myself for being a coward and not stepping into the middle of that and taking the beatings for her. I did not protect Lyndsay that day.

Lyndsay could not sit for days. Neither of us ever reported this event.

The upshot of this event was, Lyndsay never got another beating in the remainder of the time we were at the E's farm, and I think I did not either. My adult mind speculates that the event frightened even them.

As we grew older, the invasion of privacy became an even greater issue. And on this subject, I will speak only for myself, because Lyndsay's story frequently changes on this subject.

There are times Lyndsay has stated very clearly that she was subject to *unwelcome advances* of the same degree as I have disclosed, and then later, she acutely recants.

After years of her disclosing and then recanting, she began blaming me. She began stating that she would just begin to get past it, and then I would dredge it all back upon her.

I still have the card that she sent me in about 1992, blaming me for her inability to get over it and get on with her life.

At this time, it has been about twenty years since I have spoken to Lyndsay, with the exception of a few hours after one of the foster-sister's funeral.

If she was correct in her accusations of me, then I can happily rest in my heart with joy for her because that would mean that she has had twenty years of peace and healing.

I rather doubt it, but I hope the best for her. Because if it was all my influence, well—she's been free of that for two decades. Be well, my little sister!

Now, I will speak solely about me. This is my story; it is demanding a voice. It is part of my healing by shucking the disgusting memories like filthy rags.

When I was about age twelve, the importance of spying through the air vent hole and having to hide in the closet began to take on an uglier turn.

Is it possible, if I had just allowed him voyeur access, that it would have satisfied his more indecent and depraved appetites? Or is that simply my misguided sense of guilt and shame? For years I blamed myself – or correctly, I cast the blame on a child of ten through seventeen years of age. Me.

As I began to develop breasts, Mr. E became more and more—attentive. By the time my budding breasts required my first bra, Mr. E had developed a perverse attraction to them.

It started with embarrassing bumping…assertive brushing…to touching…an elbow pushed out at just the right moment to brush against my breasts…to fondling, within the short time span of months. I was embarrassed and ashamed of my breasts, and I walked around the house hunched over, my shoulders turned inward, hiding my chest.

As with the outhouse, it became a perverted cat and mouse game, where indeed I was the mouse, with full knowledge that it was no game. It was humiliating. It was relentless. I lived in a state of hypervigilance and fear at all times. From the moment I got off the school bus at the gate until I got back on the school bus the next day—it was never-ending and relentless. There was no place on the farm that I was safe.

If I were sitting at the desk in the rumpus room doing my homework and heard him sneaking down the stairs, I would run into the bedroom and close the door. Too many times, he would sneak up on me, and then I would be subjected to fondling, while he breathed deep down my neck or pushed his hard-on against my body.

He was disgusting, and he was relentless, even brazen at times. He would fondle me when I was washing the supper dishes, with Lyndsay standing beside me, drying the dishes, and Mrs. E in the next room watching TV. He would stand there with his hands in my pants, and his hard-on pushed between my butt cheeks. I would hold onto the butcher knife in the hot soapy water and will myself to spin around and stab him. I did not.

When I was about ten years old, Mr. E asked me what my favorite candy was. Without hesitation, I told him it was caramels. Soon thereafter, he would leave a caramel in my panties or bra. Once he knew I smoked, he would leave a cigarette between my breasts or in my panties when he left.

Chore time had a schedule, and the timing was relatively precise. Cows were milked and fed, milk was separated in the upper pump house, chickens, pigs, and calves were fed. It was all on a rhythm and schedule; every day, the same.

So, at the given time, when all else was done, my last chore was to go down to the lower pump house, which was in the far perimeter of the farm, about 500 feet down a hill from the house. Again, I would scan the barnyard to see where Mr. E was.

If I could see him at a distance and he was busy, I would run to the pump house, pull the power cord to the pump, dash back to the door, lock it and run back to the upper pump house. I would be free; it was success.

But not always. Mr. E became sneakier, hiding, attempting to catch me. Sometimes it would be close, and I would fly past him and run, not stopping to lock the door. I would catch hell because he would report that I left the pump house door unlocked. I could not defend myself. My voice was long since gone.

Other times and they were frequent, I would not be so lucky. I would struggle until it was clear that I could not escape. Then I would stand rigid, with every muscle in my body clenched. He would grope and put his fingers wherever he sought. I would stand with my eyes clenched shut and squeeze my body until the blood whooshed in my ears.

The last time he caught me in the pump house, he trapped my arms in a bearhug and squeezed, trying to kiss me with his tongue slopping around in my mouth, his foul breath gagging me.

Then he sat down on a wood stump and dragged me down on top of him. He bent me backwards on his lap and stuck his hands inside my pants and forced his fingers inside me and pushed hard until it was extremely painful.

His thumb stroked my pubic hair, and he told me that the reason I had hair down there is that without it, boys would eat it. I was humiliated and disgusted. I could not move.

He was sweating profusely, and his disgusting sweat dripped on my face, his foul breath—that deep-chested steam engine breathing. He told me he wanted me so bad and that if I let him have sex with me, he would give me anything I wanted. He said he would sign over to me up to half of everything he owned, just for one time.

I heard the words like they were coming from some distant hollow place. I had my eyes squeezed shut as hard as I could. I wanted to scream; I could not. I wanted to cry; I could not. I wanted to die; I could not. I wanted to kick, punch, bite; I could not move. I wanted to kill him. I did not.

Finally, he let me go, and I ran from the pump house and never stopped until I got back to the upper yard where Mrs. E was. I felt filthy and sick. He never reported me for not locking the pump house door.

This scenario, or ones just like it repeated over and over from when I was about twelve years old until I was eighteen and finally left the farm. I tried to forget. I have never forgotten. He is dead now. I will hate him until I am dead.

I never told anyone the horror and humiliation until I was thirty-two years old, and it all spilled out of me one night, unexpectedly, to a girlfriend.

I cried for days and weeks. I threw up. I shook uncontrollably. I had a hard time functioning at work. I could not sleep. I tried counselling off and on, but I could never express it. My jaw would clamp shut.

I began experiencing migraines and nightmares. I started to feel scared and unsafe for no apparent reason.

Eventually, I sank into an abyss of self-loathing, a place where the touch of my own hand disgusted me. It was a place where only the thought of leaving my sweet innocent daughter behind kept me from ending my life.

I weighed every detail of my life, and nothing else had any value. Every dark voice snarled at me, "She would be better off without you. Don't be selfish. Give her a chance at a better life."

I began walking around with my teeth clamped shut, and my fists clenched all the time, day after day. I sank lower and lower until my family doctor prescribed medication for me.

Finally, in despair, I broke. I could not talk. When I opened my mouth, my jaw quaked and shuttered. This progressed into panic attacks until I finally collapsed into a full-blown nervous breakdown.

I could not stand being near my husband. We ended up fighting all the time. I could not speak unless I held my jaw tightly: without which my jaw would quake until the sound could not pass through my lips. I was very sick.

Finally, in desperation, I filled my prescriptions and went home. I woke my daughter and told her I loved her and I held her. I whispered, "I am sorry." I kissed her on the forehead and said goodbye.

I went upstairs and calmly poured all my medications into a glass, filled it with water, and gagged the acidy chemical brew down my throat and forced myself not to vomit.

Calmly, I walked down the stairs and climbed into bed. I told my husband I was sorry for everything and rolled over and closed my eyes.

I was beginning to fall asleep when my husband leaped out of bed and roared, "What have you done?" He threw the light on and roared it again.

I told him nothing and told him to go to sleep.

He was silent for about a minute, then he grabbed me out of bed and dragged me to the bathroom. He forced his fingers down my throat repeatedly. He told me God told him what I had done.

He dragged me out of the house to the car and drove like a madman across the city to the emergency ward of the hospital with the four-way flashers on.

Shortly after we got to the hospital, I lost consciousness. I remember the emergency staff roughly waking me up and making me drink something. I lost consciousness. I remember them forcing a tube down my nose into my stomach. I remember them yelling, "swallow, swallow." I lost consciousness.

I remember slowly floating to the surface, trying to reach my nose with my hand. My nose was terribly itchy. My hands were tied down. In my attempt to scratch my nose, they deemed me to be combative. Perhaps I was.

They put medications in me to make me vomit and others to make my bowels move. I remember seeing lots of black stuff. I remember flashes of things that left me with a profound feeling of humiliation.

The next morning, I remember starting to come around, drifting up toward a light. I could feel someone's hand fondling my right breast. I sharply came to and began trying to ward the hands off of me. As I opened my eyes, there was a man that I did not know and never saw again.

He said, "Oh, good. You are awake. I will let them know." He abruptly left.

I was sick with humiliation and a sense of violation.

I was admitted to the psych ward of the hospital for a few days. It was during my stay at the psych ward that I replayed all the events of that night over and over in my head. I made a firm decision that I would never entertain suicide again. I never have.

Although, perhaps suicidal thoughts and behavior may have been replaced by self-mutilation, cutting, and whipping myself with belts until I bled, all in an attempt to stop the dead feeling and make myself feel something – even if it is pain.

This had not been my first suicide attempt, but it was perhaps the closest I came to completion. I did not know that it was not normal to think of suicide. I thought of death and suicide every day of my life.

My first attempt was when I was about six years old. I was almost successful. I tried to strangle myself in the barn. No one ever knew, but it was so very close that time. I had tightened the wool scarf so tight around my neck, and as I was passing out, I struggled to untie it, but the knot was too tight.

I would have been found in the milk cows' feed manger while they ate their hay around my body.

Another serious attempt was when I was fifteen. I took a handful of pills from the medicine cabinet. I was really spaced out and depressed on the school bus the following morning. My girlfriend asked me what was wrong. She reported me to the school guidance counsellor. I must ask. Why was this never investigated?

So many times, the Department of Child Welfare had glaring signs that there was much trouble in paradise, but not once did they intervene. The school did not. The police did not. The neighbors and family members that knew there was a big problem did not. No one blew the whistle.

Chapter 9 — Healing

There were tens of thousands of Aboriginal and Métis children apprehended in the Sixties Scoop. I know others have gone through what I did or much worse, and my heart has a message for you. Your heart may resonate with the words on these pages. If so, then this book was written for you as much as for me.

There are shocking similarities in many of the Scoopers' stories. Who wrote the rule book on how these kids could or should be treated?

Your wounds are real. Your healing journey is yours, and it is as unique as you. As long as you persist and persevere, to stand up one more time, dust off the worn knees of your jeans, step forward and are willing to do it one more time, you will find a place of peace inside.

Understand that the word *healing* connotes a process. I believe that there is such a thing as miraculous healing, which connotes an instantaneous occurrence, and truly, all healing is a miracle.

But most often, we work out every infliction, whatever the cause may have been. It is in the process of working through things that we learn coping skills and healing strategies that precipitate our own healing that we can share with others.

Often in my adult years, I would inwardly cry out in pain and suffering and wonder what the hell was so wrong with me that I could not get my life on track. I often suffered periods of deep crushing emotional pain, unidentifiable in origin; therefore, for me, that was much scarier. It was like my brain would be on fire. It was as if it was smoldering and grinding round and round until it was like missing cogs in a wheel. My brain would begin to slip.

Sometimes it would start with one insignificant incident, and it would morph into consuming darkness that swallowed everything – except the smile I perpetually pasted on my face.

I would endure long periods of anguish, torment, and bouts of depression over life situations.

Oh, my life looked pretty much OK from the outside, I think. I held responsible jobs and excelled. I excelled in education. But no one really ever knew the torment that I lived with inside, or the shame I carried with me of the knowledge of who I was – not white.

My fight and flight responses were so overly exaggerated – I would jump and scream at things that others hardly noticed.

One large event can cause a cracking or fracturing in our psyche resulting in post-traumatic stress disorder (PTSD). Science and mental health practitioners tell us that years of systematic abuse, repeated over and over, may result in the same thing.

When I about thirty-six years old and living in Kelowna with my husband B, I was quietly standing at the kitchen sink with my hands in the hot soapy water, my thoughts floating away freely. B had entered the kitchen behind me without me hearing him. He leaned against my back and reached around me and put his hands around my breasts. My mind snapped. I had the butcher knife in my hand and would have stabbed B if he had not been so quick to respond. For weeks, I agonized about how close that came to tragedy. I wondered how I would have ever been able to explain that to defense counsel, a judge, or a jury.

I was suffering from PTSD and had no idea. A thought, a memory, a sound, a touch, to see a similar physique, hear a similar voice, a smell...could send me into an emotional decline so deep, that several times I suffered from full-blown nervous breakdowns that took a year or two to recover from fully. And except for a few weeks at the beginning of such a decline, with medication I still functioned. I went to work, I dealt with the public, I completed my duties, I attended university classes, I maintained my household duties, and I was still a mom and a wife.

I think that it was my spouses and my daughter, who suffered the most. Everyone else was free to walk away when the going got tough.

Along with the emotional upheaval, were illnesses: phantom pain that fired all over my body like an electrical storm, extraordinarily poor baby teeth, migraines, irritable bowel syndrome (IBS), stomach aches, continuous muscle aches and pain, chronic inflammation with no discernable cause, sleep disorders, night terrors, continuous bronchial and sinus problems, rheumatoid arthritis. What was normal for me was abnormal! I can remember crying out and saying, "I just want to be normal!" I did not know what normal was, but I knew it sure as hell was not me.

I've had very great doctors over the years, but no one could get to the bottom of the myriad of ailments and problems. I went for counselling, and no one was able to dig deep enough to find the bottom of my well. But when I hit the bottom of the well, I never allowed myself to stay there. I prayed and researched and read, sought counsel, turned introspective, and examined myself.

Remember, ever since I was a four-year-old child, I knew those bad things were my fault. So, I would always look at myself first. It was during one such episode of searching that I was given a revelation: a parable from God, that instructed me and gave me a roadmap, or tool to the discovery of inner healing. I was shown the following.

"A Parable of Healing"

Our heart is like a garden—it is the garden of our soul. In the center of our garden is a tree. It is a tree that is uniquely ours.

In the corner of your garden, there is a compost heap. All the hurtful, destructive things that have happened to you have been thrown into the compost heap.

All our mistakes and the destructive actions and words of others end up on that spot in your heart—the place inside of you that nurses and rehearses every detail and finds you a victim. You won't see it on an x-ray, but you know where it is.

Some folks have small hurts and normal growing issues, and when those things are laid on the compost heap in the garden of their hearts, they just decompose.

But sometimes one's life is replete with circumstances so abundant and devastating that when they were thrown on the compost heap in the corner of our hearts, they were not given the appropriate time or attention to complete the decomposition process. Some of the events were too big, and sometimes there are just too many events. It is quite the same.

Sometimes, that old head of lettuce no longer looks like lettuce. We should be thoughtfully accurate about what issue is being revealed or exposed, requiring our attention at that specific time, so we are dealing with the right fundamental issue. If it looks like mush but is really slimy lettuce, perhaps it needs to be placed in a different spot in your garden.

Sometimes, it just doesn't matter – it just needs to be dealt with and laid on the soil of the garden. Recognize it. Deal with it. Do not be afraid of it. That old circumstance or event cannot hurt you today, except when you nurse it and rehearse it.

Some of us have a huge pile of rotting and stinking matter piled up. We need to go through that pile and pull it apart.

Issue by issue, we deal with each thing, and then we lay it on the soil in the garden of your heart.

That issue then disintegrates and becomes fertilizer for your tree in the center of your garden. The nutrients go down into the soil and feed your tree.

Your tree becomes strong and bears fruit. As others pass by your garden, some stop in to assist you in cleaning up your compost heap. Some pass by, see the fruit, and it is exactly what they need to nourish their soul so they can continue on their journey.

***

In my journey for healing and wholeness, I found an amazing research project that was conducted in Dunedin, New Zealand[4]. It was the pivotal point in my life for healing and change in my soul and helped me to understand the myriad of physical ailments and conditions that swirled around me like a fog from as early as four years of age.

So phenomenal and so encompassing this study is, that I believe that it is the single greatest gift I can offer you as a reader, whether it is for your own healing, or to help you to understand what someone you love is struggling with. I pray that you will use the footnote link and read the study.

---

[4] Dunedin Longitudinal Study, The Dunedin Multidisciplinary Health and Development Study: overview of the first 40 years, with an eye to the future

I have shared my early childhood experiences, and the devastation that resulted in my life, and my steps toward a healed and happy life. But I recommend The Dunedin Study to all survivors of the Sixties Scoop in particular and all survivors of early childhood trauma in general.

Multidisciplinary research into how early childhood trauma affected the victims across their life span was undertaken beginning in 1972. It is considered to be the most comprehensive study of its kind, ever, because of its breadth and its depth. The Dunedin Study, as it is commonly referred to, has released over 1,200 research papers, of which about 60% are peer-reviewed.

There have been thousands of studies initiated worldwide since that time, to garner even greater insight into how certain traumatic experiences in the early life of a child, and familial crises and poverty, affects things like the physical and mental health, the learning ability, and the psychosocial functioning of the victim of early childhood trauma.

In the Dunedin Study, over one thousand children born in the early seventies were followed and studied for about forty years.

Each participant was questioned very carefully and thoroughly about their socioeconomic circumstances, their learning ability, their ability to flourish in social settings, education, careers, and their mental and physical health, and so on. A clinical psychologist was hired to assess the participant's mental health, dentist for dental assessments, and medical personnel for medical laboratory tests and coronary stress tests.

The results of this study are staggering and insightful. As I researched on the study: watching videos, and Ted Talks, reading research papers and reports, following peer-reviewed commentaries, and some marvelous studies that came off of this study, I began to understand why my life seemed to be in recurring upheaval, emotionally and physically.

I began to understand in greater depth how specific situations of abuse and general circumstances such as constant hyper-vigilance spanning years, constant fear, parentification issues, and never-ending stress and anxiety, created devastating complications in my physical, emotional, and mental health.

With all the stress as described earlier in this book and the stress-related stomach issues that I had even before I got to the foster home, I think it is understandable that I developed a lot of stomach related health issues and IBS later in life.

I had constant sore throats, bad cough after a bad cough. My young body was unable to cope with the heightened levels of stress. Every school outing or party where there were anticipation and excitement building up to it, I would miss it because I would end up sick. Even the stress of good events was an overload to my system.

I was subject to extreme cases of cold sores that covered the exterior of my mouth for about a half-inch around my lips, covered my lips, up inside my nose, covered the inside of my mouth and down into my esophagus and windpipe. The doctor I was taken to was horrified at the extent of the plague. I had recurring bouts of cold sores my entire childhood.

I was hospitalized in grade two to have all my baby teeth removed because my teeth were in such bad condition.

I had constant stomach aches so bad that I would mix vinegar and baking soda for relief. I never received medical attention for this.

I had severe problems with endometriosis from the onset of puberty. Although I was incapacitated from menstrual pain for several days, at the onset of every cycle, I was never taken for medical help for it. There was no sympathy or compassion for the condition. I still completed my chores as best I could.

As I continued to learn more about the long-term effects of early childhood trauma, I began to see that it was not "me" who was abnormal, per se. It was not "me" who was a human wasteland. It was situations and circumstances from which I was subjected as a little girl that was abnormal. When these things were happening to me, I was too young to guard myself, and it was inappropriate for anyone to expect that of me. I did not fail myself; the adults around me failed me.

As I moved forward in healing, I began to understand the difference between "me" and the things that happened to me.

It was liberating. I was able to come to a sincere place of peace within myself, knowing and accepting who I am. I am Métis – why had that been so difficult to get out of my mouth? The more I insist on respectful treatment from others and am less demanding of myself, I gain liberty and healing.

Today, by just retelling my story, I become ill with headaches, body pain, crushing fatigue, stomach pain, and increased bowel pain and diarrhea. I anticipate the day, soon, where even those effects will be diminished.

I was able to look at my life and circumstances from a more objective and analytical perspective, rather than just the emotional reaction to triggers and stimuli that I had been trapped in previously.

From this different perspective and with greater insight, I was able to peel away the detritus in my compost heap, and with the help of dear friends and sometimes strangers, I was able to lay some of that on the garden of my heart where it has benefited my life and the lives of others.

It is my great hope that survivors of the Sixties Scoop who have suffered the harrowing devastation in their lives can find a key to unlock their torment and find peace and healing, as well.

I further hope that the friends and family of Sixties Scoop victims who read this story will find some understanding of what happened to their loved one under the social welfare system. And through that understanding, find compassion and the strength to forgive what seems to be great inconsistencies and incongruencies in their lives.

I have always seen this dilemma from my perspective as a scooper. Recently, I have come to understand that my experience has, in turn, caused deep pain to my loved ones. I am grieved by that notion. I hope this helps a little.

***

I have learned a great truth about Marlene's actions upon my life. Marlene represents the condemnation of maternal rejection. Racism and poverty are valid excuses for Marlene.

I have learned a great truth and gained great insight into maternal instinct and demonstration of familial love and have come to recognize the condemnation that belongs to Mrs. E, not me. Familial mental health may be a valid excuse for Mrs. E.

I have learned great truth and achieved deep understanding, healing, and restoration from the perversion of love, and resolved, in fact, to settle that condemnation at Mr. E's feet. I hold him in legal and moral contempt and without excuse.

What I have learned about the results of the apprehension of my siblings and me are:

1) The government had the primary responsibility for the apprehension of my siblings and me and, according to my Social Welfare file, did so without legal just cause and certainly not meeting the *Best Interests of the Child Test*.

2) The Department of Child Welfare in the province of Alberta in 1959 was negligent in their *duty of care* regarding my siblings and me by failing to adequately screen the people whose home they placed me into and whom they paid a monthly wage and all our living expenses. Poverty was a major factor in the situation Marlene found herself in, and rather than putting a little bit of money into Marlene's household so she could keep her family together, they chose to throw the money into the foster care program.

3) The Department of Child Welfare in the province of Alberta failed to conduct adequate ongoing follow-up with my siblings and me, whereby jeopardizing our safety, and therein creating an atmosphere in which our victimizers could operate with impunity.

4) The Department of Child Welfare in the province of Alberta failed to investigate significant events that were brought to their attention, to protect my siblings and me.

As a result of their actions in some situations and their lack of actions in others it is my opinion that the condemnation of the destruction of my family and the lives of my siblings and me, wards of the government and under their care and control, rests at the feet of a heartless government with a vile agenda against her Aboriginal peoples. I am unable to provide any plausible excuse for the actions of the Department of Child Welfare. The government has never seen fit to offer any excuse or apology to me, or the Sixties Scoop victims of the Métis Nation or their families and communities.

In the 1960s, although the Aboriginal population in Alberta was about 10%, they made up about 69% of children in care in the Department of Child Welfare. Métis children were six times more likely to be foster kids than white kids. Poverty was a major factor in apprehensions.

***

A country, strong and free? Canada declares itself on the world stage as a First World, peacekeeping progressive and humanitarian country. This is the same country where Aboriginal women are missing, murdered, and forgotten by society, only remembered by their families and communities.

If this were white women who were disappearing and/or murdered at the same rate, there would be an outcry that would rock this country and would be condemned by every country in the world.

Because it is Aboriginal women whom we are talking about here, it is a story that we stumble upon in a Google search or that crops up for a few days when another girl goes missing, or another body is found.

It is my opinion that millions upon billions of dollars would become available instantly to stop that madness if the Aboriginal victims were wrapped in the skin of a different color and came from a different cultural background.

What I am saying is, this is a systemic problem. And it cannot be fixed by saying, "we are sorry." It is going to require real actions, and genuine and constructive change.

All too often, another story of a missing or murdered Aboriginal girl or woman is brought to our attention in the media, is met with a roll of their eyes, a sneer, or a condemning comment of blaming the victim. Somehow it is just another Indian problem—those people.

All too often, I have heard the coarse and ignorant comments. They make me want to scream. It is atrocious, and it is unacceptable.

I understand that there is a political voice out there that walks a diplomatic line, careful not to cause too great a stir, not to awaken the sleeping bear. Not just one political party or another, but a systemic voice.

I reckon that voice needs to be silenced, and a new voice needs to be raised with strength, admitting guilt with honesty and full disclosure. A voice that does not mince words, but one that takes responsibility. The things that were done in political secret need to be shouted from the rooftops…shouted in the legislature…shouted in the parliament…shouted in the closed-door meeting and the negotiations.

Because every victim of the Sixties Scoop, whether they are the victims that the courts have acknowledged, or the ones that have yet to have their claims heard and redressed, condemns the actions of the Government of Canada. Not by the victims' outrage, but by the very act of covering up the issue and refusing to acknowledge the crimes perpetrated against untold thousands of Indian, Inuit, and Métis children and families, the government condemns itself.

Chapter 10 — I am Métis

I sometimes wonder what the point is of all of this labor of verbally vomiting the horrors of my childhood out on these pages. I think about why I have dredged up and fought through every painful memory and laid some of it out on these pages.

Often just telling the story, or in writing it here, it would make me physically sick, and I would have to retire to my bed for a day or two, or close myself in the bathroom and soak in the tub with candles glowing – and go numb.

Some stories and memories will not rest until they are told. Some voices cannot be stopped until they are heard. Lies do not evaporate. Truth cannot flourish if it is never spoken. And healing does not happen in a vacuum. Shame and humiliation cannot be vanquished from a victim's heart when they lie in the shadows fed by secrets.

It is for me to understand: to put it into perspective the hell I went through, to end the secrecy that has trapped me in a cycle of self-loathing and despair, falsely accusing myself and taking on the blame that belonged to someone else – the adults.

It is to set free a little girl who has been locked up inside of me and suffocated under layers and layers of lies and false accusations, traumatized by guilt, shame, humiliation, hyper-vigilance, degradation, and abandonment.

It is for me to see it for what it truthfully was so I could absolve myself of the blame and shame and humiliation that was never mine to carry in the first place. Layer by layer, I peel through the debris and detritus, the garbage and the wreckage, that was my life.

In doing so, I heal. And through my healing, it is my hope that others will also find healing.

It was time for me to find the courage to unburden that little girl who lived in a withered state in a dark and horrid place and set her free.

Now, I sit beside her with my arm around her shoulders. I tell her I am sorry I was not there to protect her. I assure her that I am now. We became friends. It is time to go on and live in peace, with dignity and freedom, and create myself a healthy self-image.

I am done being silent and protecting the guilty with my silence. I trust that this statement is heard. I have done what I can to "protect" the identity of the guilty, but I will not be held accountable for one more day to protect them with my silence at the expense of my health and well-being. If you were not there – then you do not know! I was there.

I grew up in a white world, in a white community, with middle class religious white foster parents, and I was educated in a white school. None of that made me white. Understanding that, was the key to unlocking the shame that I was indoctrinated to believe over a decade and a half of dismantling my cultural identity. I was told that I should embrace the opportunity I was given to fit into the white society.

When I was a teenager and a young adult, I wanted to be white, much like Marlene did, I think. We wanted to be seen as white because there was favor there, and without that connection to "white", I felt worthless. I had been raised to believe that to be anything but white was dirty and, in all ways, "less than."

I have been told how fortunate I was to have been taken away from my mother and that I should be grateful for the opportunity to be raised in a middle-class white home in a white community. I have been judged by these people as ungrateful for the handout given me. These people know of folks in their own family who were foster parents, and I have been instructed on the profound virtues of white benevolence of foster parents who give their all for the good of troubled children.

I am not against foster parenting in general. I just believe that if the government steps in to disrupt a family, then they must be as aggressive with protecting those children once they are in their care. I also believe that maintaining familial, cultural, and community ties are paramount in the mental health of a child.

I have been out of the foster care system for over forty-five years. I am an intelligent and fair-minded adult on the positive side of the healing curve. When I weigh out the good, the bad, and the ugly of Marlene and the foster parents, I still cannot claim that the foster home was better for me. It was not. There were other options available, just not entertained by the government.

Some people think that it was just a well-meaning government department with a few misguided policies, attempting to do good. Where is the evidence of that in my file, I wonder?

I have stated in the past that I grew up feeling like a baby pig that had been taken out of the barn and raised in the house. I no longer belonged in the barn, but I sure as hell did not belong in the house.

I had been thoroughly stripped of identity. I will not say that it was an intentional plot against me to make me feel not Métis and not white – but rootless. Still, it is impossible for a foster parent or social worker not to impart their colonial mindset onto impressionable children.

I want to say that again – so important it is. It is impossible for an authority figure in the life of an impressionable child not to create or cause cultural mentality, whereby the child struggles with shame and identity issues when it comes from a place of colonial supremacy—hence, the fundamental and paramount urgency for culturally-based foster care. The primary concern here is that it creates decades of confusion in the child and causes barriers to healing and healthy self-image, as adults.

I think that a feeling of not belonging anywhere has been a fundamental problem for me – popping up in many forms throughout my life, and the blockage from healing in my life. Casting off the shame of who I am, was the key to finding a place to belong.

Some folks actually think I am lucky – they see it as my having two families – a great abundance of belonging. That could not be further from the truth. I had no family.

I have struggled for several decades with acknowledging my Métis blood. Confused, I would step out of the white world and then retreat back into it.

I found my mom – I stepped out.

I rejected my mom – I stepped back.

Back and forth, I struggled throughout my life, a small paper ship at the mercy of the waves and wind.

I believe that I needed to find myself – the strength of my blood – my truth – my heritage – my family, for me to have a safe place to sit down and address my past and unpack my shame that I carried around with me like an old suitcase

In April 2019, I attended the last of the six Engagement Sessions put on by the Métis Nation British Columbia and the Métis National Council for Métis Survivors of the Sixties Scoop in Richmond, British Columbia,

It was with a profound sense of disconnection from everything that I made my way through the doors of the Engagement Session. I had spent sixty-four years sliding through life like a greased fish, trying to find purpose somewhere in a relationship, in a family, or an organization.

I entered the conference room and sat in the very front. In the opening Ceremonies, Frances Chartrand spoke about the dark era in our nation's collective history and the trauma experienced by the forced separation of Métis Nation children from their families.

I was riveted to every word proceeding from her mouth. Every single word she spoke was specifically for me. Every word was like a sharp knife that reached inside of me and began to cut away the shackles and cords that bound me up on the inside, way back from that first day in the summer of 1959, when the two social workers arrived at Auntie Jean's house and took three frightened Métis children away from their family.

Frances Chartrand looked straight into my eyes and ended with the words, "You are Métis, and you are home."

I cannot explain with mere words the miracle that transpired inside of me in that precise moment. It was like I unzipped. It was like I turned inside right, and for the first time in my life, I knew I had come home and that I belonged.

The final ceremony of the weekend was a "Sash Ceremony." The Métis Nation BC honored the Sixties Scoop attendees by welcoming us home and presenting us with our first Métis symbol – the Métis Sash. I was one of the later ones called to the front of the room to be honored. Again, my stomach was in knots, maybe they will not call my name…so afraid that just as I found a place to belong, it would be torn away.

They called my name. It was like a dream. I remember them placing the sash over my shoulders and speaking soothing kind words to me. It doesn't even matter to me what the words were, I could not hear them through my tears and emotion – my spirit heard them clearly.

Since that day, and through the process of acknowledging and claiming my heritage and culture, through the process of researching genealogical records, I have found my grandmother's story, my mother's story, and I have found some of Marlene's living relatives.

In this process, I have struggled to access my records and documents in my search to find my family and cultural roots. It seems fundamentally wrong to me that the government that undertook the fiduciary *duty of care* and control over my life, insisting they could do better for me than my family, but failed me so miserably and completely should be able to dictate to me what records I am entitled to.

At the very least, I feel that the governments of Alberta and Canada owe me the assistance I need to reconnect with family, culture, and community that they separated me from, and to help heal the great wounds they caused me and my loved ones, through their negligence.

The genealogist for the Métis Nation BC helped me to get some of my records, and I have now been able to trace my genealogy back around 250 years.

It is a marvel! A thrill! For a little girl that could not even look back as far as to remember her mother's face, and did not know her father's name, to seeing names and reading stories about my bloodline – now talking in terms of centuries. I give my head a slight shake, and I smile!

In early September, I received a package in the mail. I am now a proud member of the Métis Nation! I received my Métis membership card and certificate. I will admit now the fear I carried all summer, that once again, I would be let down, and I would not be accepted into the Métis community.

The smile on my face today is from my heart. I am Métis! I say that with pride!

Today, I am living a healthier, happier life. My smile is genuine. I am proud of the amazing reclamation and reconciliation of my life. It did not come from the pain I suffered in my life – but from my inner strength and resilience – the guts to continue to stand in the center of my human condition – in honor of my Métis heritage – the blood in my veins.

Marsee – Pishshapmishko
Thank you – Take care

KP Rogers

Behind the Smile

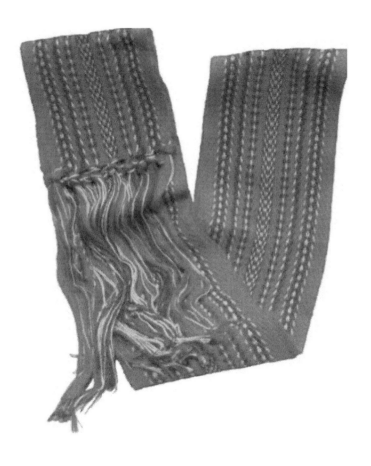

Bibliography

Abandoned Litter – We were not legally abandoned. I (KP Rogers) have a copy of my Department of Child Welfare file, and in 2019 I had a career Social Worker read it. It is clear from my file that there were no legal grounds for apprehension, at least under the social workers' policies and procedures today. If this event occurred today, we would never have been removed from Marlene's custody.

Dunedin Longitudinal Study: The Dunedin Multidisciplinary Health and Development Study. Overview of the first forty years, with an eye to the future. https://dunedinstudy.otago.ac.nz/

Graham, Mr. and Mrs. – Pseudonym has been used throughout this book.

Johnston, Patrick. 1983. Native Children in the Child Welfare System. Ottawa: Canadian Council on Social Development.

Lyndsay – Pseudonym has been used throughout this book.

About the Author

KP Rogers raised her daughter and once she left the nest to embark on her own dreams, it was time to turn her mind toward her own dreams. She completed her Bachelor of Law at the University of Victoria, BC, Faculty of Law as an adult student.

KP Rogers lives with her partner Jack in British Columbia, Canada during the summers keeping up with her daughter, son-in-law, two wonderful grandsons – the loves of their lives, and a great-grandson – the treasures of her life. She winters in Costa Rica, where she has taken up bird watching, painting, coloring, and writing as Therapeutic Creative Release.

KP Rogers enjoys the adventures of exploring new territory by horseback, quad, or car in both countries she calls home. Her full-time pursuit is creating peace in her life.

Marsee and Pura Vida.

You can contact KP at kp.rogers.bts@gmail.com

Manufactured by Amazon.ca
Bolton, ON

28471200R00087